Tadpoles & Tiddlers

THIRTY TWO KNITTING DESIGNS FOR BABIES AND CHILDREN UP TO TEN YEARS

A ROWAN PRODUCTION

To Hilary and David

Copyright © Rowan Yarns 1995

First published in Great Britain in 1995 by
Rowan Yarns Ltd
Green Lane Mill
Holmfirth
West Yorkshire
England
HD7 1RW

Editor Kathleen Hargreaves
Photographed by Joey Toller
Design and Styling by Kim Hargreaves and Louisa Harding
Hair & Makeup Adrienne Atkinson
Design layout Les Dunford
Knitting co-ordinator Elizabeth Armitage
Pattern checker Catherine Cummings

British Library Cataloguing in Publication Data
Rowan Yarns
Tadpoles and Tiddlers
1. Knitting - patterns
I. Title
ISBN 0 9525375 0 8

Printed by Raithby, Lawrence & Company Ltd
De Montfort Press
Slater Street
Leicester LE3 5AY

Contents

"Tadpoles . . .

Back row from left to right, Charlotte wears Sampler sweater, Joe wears McTavish jacket, Beth
Front row from left to right, Zoe wears Checker jacket, Meggie wears Cuddle cardigan, Alice wears

... & Tiddlers"

wears Odd Job sweater, Holly wears Mr Pepper sweater and Kate wears Hearts and Flowers sweater.
Nann jacket, Grace wears Sailor Sam sweater, Jack wears Cuddle sweater and Sam wears Riddler jacket.

"Meggie and Charlotte were pleased with what they had gathered from their vegetable garden"

Meggie is wearing Mary Mary cardigan, page 84, Charlotte is wearing Queen of Hearts sweater, page 46.

"Daisy in her Sunday best"

Daisy is wearing Busy Lizzie cardigan, page 65.

"Shh! Keep quiet, I thought I heard someone coming"

Daisy wears Bobby sweater, page 64, Meredith wears Milly Mop cardigan, page 69.

"Michael felt very left out as he was not allowed an apple"

Micheal is wearing Bobby sweater, page 64, lying on Patchwork blanket, page 56.

"We'll have these finished in no time !"

Zoe wears Sea Shanty sweater, page 45, Ella wears Sweetheart sweater, page 50

Hang on tight !!!, we're coming to a bumpy bit now"

Zoe is wearing Garden Patchwork sweater, page 49, Sam is wearing Fisherman sweater, page 78.

"Thursday was market day"

Alice is wearing Moby sweater, page 68 and Bonnie hat, Daisy is wearing Milly Mop cardigan, page 69.

"Daisy and Meridith felt very grown up in their summer cardigans"

Daisy is wearing Mary Mary cardigan, page 84, Meredith is wearing Primrose cardigan, page 58.

Michael felt grown up too"

Michael wears Hamish jacket, page 66 and Jelly hat, lying on Mrs McHugh's blanket, page 61

"Alexander and Teddy were best of friends"

Alexander wears Fish sweater, page 53.

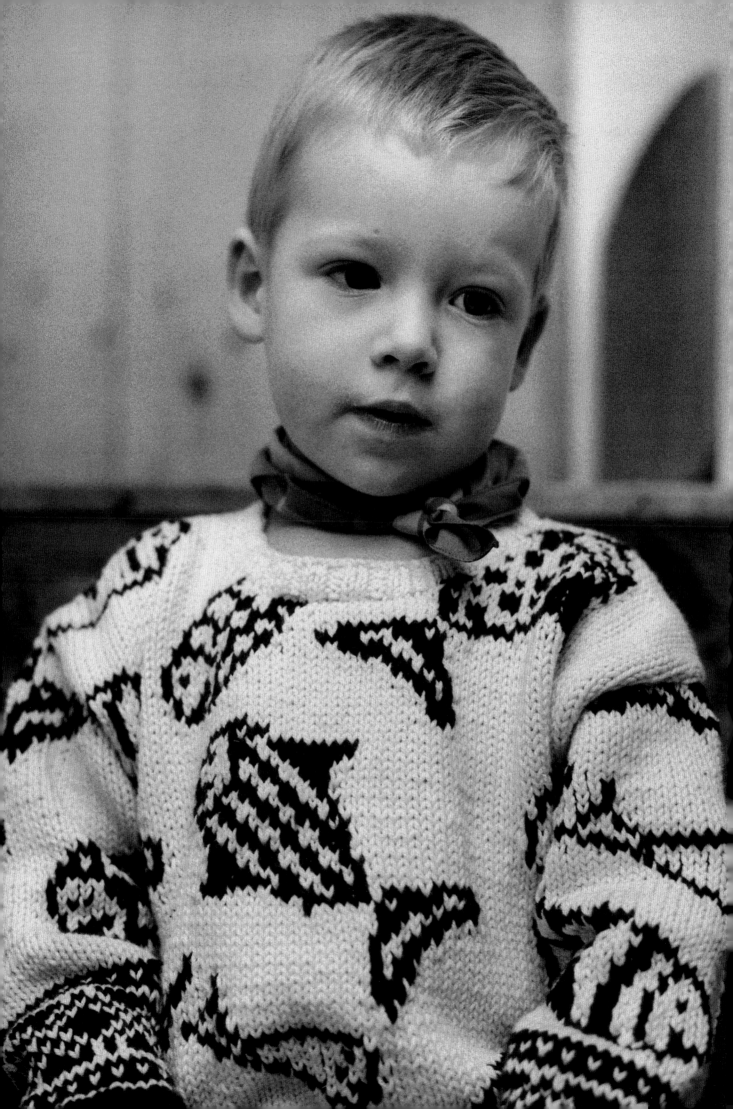

"I'm the King of the castle, get away from me you rascal"
Daniel wears Jammy Dodger sweater, page 54.

"Meggie was checking to see if Jack Frost had got her flowers"

Meggie is wearing Lazy Daisy sweater, page 42.

"It's not bedtime yet, is it?"

Maddie is wearing Queen of Hearts sweater, page 46.

"Who's for a story ?"

Alexander wears Jack Flash jacket, page 40.

"That's a good noise Charlie!"

Charlie is wearing Checker jacket, page 44, Harry is wearing Pee Wee sweater, page 77.

"Beth was off to her secret hiding place"

Beth is wearing Fire Cracket jacket, page 41 and Bonnie hat.

"The trunk was full of treasure"

Leoni is wearing Cuddle sweater, page 59, Liane is wearing Nann jacket, page 74.

"Joe was first in to bat"

Joe wears McTavish jacket, page 79.

"Homeward bound, after a hard day at school"

Liane is wearing Highlander jacket, page 63 and Jelly hat.

"A man's work is never done!"

Charlie wears Odd Job jacket, page 48.

"Whhheeeeee!!!!!!"

Joe wears Pie Man sweater, page 76, Charlotte wears Sailor Sam sweater, page 75.

"Alice and Kate took it in turns to ride Fudge"

Alice wears McTavish jacket, page 79, Kate wears How jacket, page 70.

"Georgia, the snowman's getting cold!"

Lily is wearing Riddler jacket, page 55, Piper scarf and mitts.

"You could lend him your scarf !"

Georgia is wearing Highlander jacket, page 63 and mitts.

"Only the older children . . .

Back row from left to right, Jack wears Riddler jacket, Joe wears Pie Man sweater,
Front row from left to right, Grace wears Mr Pepper sweater, Meggie wears How jacket,

. . . were allowed on this expedition"

Holly wears Highlander jacket and Charlotte wears Mr Pepper sweater.
Alice wears McTavish, Kate wears Sampler sweater and Beth wears Moby sweater.

"Can you see home from here Charlotte?"

Charlotte is wearing Mr Pepper sweater, page 53 and Jelly hat, Kate is wearing Sampler sweater, page 72 and Gooseberry hat.

"Jack was expedition leader"

Jack wears Riddler jacket, page 55 and Jelly hat.

"Watch out !, here comes a snowball !!!"

Charlie wears Fire Cracker sweater, page 41.

The Knitting Patterns

"It had been a wonderful day."

Jack Flash

by KIM HARGREAVES

YARNS

Rowan Handknit D.K. Cotton

A Ecru	251	2(2:3:3:3:4:5:5:5)	50gm
B Black	252	2(2:3:3:3:3:4:4:4)	50gm
C Diana	287	3(3:4:4:4:5:5:6:6)	50gm

Sizes

1st(2nd:3rd:4th:5th:6th:7th:8th:9th)

To fit

6mth(9mth:1-2:2-3:3-4:4-6:6-8:8-9:9-10) yrs

Actual width

29.5(32.5:35.5:38.5:41.5:44.5:47.5:51.5:55.5)cm
11¹/₂(12¹/₂:14:15¹/₂:16¹/₂:17¹/₂:18¹/₂:20¹/₂:22)ins]

Length

29(32:35:38:41:44:47:51:55)cm
[11¹/₂(12¹/₂:13¹/₂:15:16¹/₂:17¹/₂:18¹/₂:20:21¹/₂) ins]

Sleeve length

19(20:23:25:28:30.5:35.5:38:40.5)cm
[7¹/₂(8:9:9¹/₂:11:12:14:15:16)ins]

NEEDLES

1 pair 3¹/₄mm (no 10) (US 3) needles
1 pair 4mm (no 8) (US 6) needles

BUTTONS 6(6:6:6:7:7:7:8:8)

TENSION

20 sts and 28 rows to 10cm measured over
stocking stitch using 4mm (US 6) needles

BACK

Cast on 51(57:63:69:75:81:87:93:101) sts
using 3¹/₄mm (US 3) needles and yarn A.
Work in **moss stitch** as folls:
Row 1: (K1, P1) to last st, K1.
Rep this row 5(5:5:5:5:5:7:7:7) times more.
Change to 4mm (US 6) needles and cont in st
st in stripe sequence as folls:
Row 1 (RS): K using A.
Row 2: P using A.
Row 3: K using B.
Row 4: P using B.
These 4 rows form the patt and are rep
throughout the back.
Keeping patt correct inc 1 st at each end of
next row and 3(3:3:3:3:3:3:4:4) foll 10th
rows.
(59(65:71:77:83:89:95:103:111)sts)
Cont without further shaping until work
measures 29(32:35:38:41:44:47:51:55)cm
from cast on edge ending with a WS row.
Shape shoulders and back neck
Keeping colour sequence correct, cast off
6(7:8:9:10:10:11:12:13) sts at beg of next 2
rows.
Cast off 6(7:8:9:10:10:11:12:13) sts, knit
11(12:12:13:13:15:15:16:17), turn leaving
rem sts on a holder.
Work each side of neck separately.
Cast off 4 sts, work to end.
Cast off rem 7(8:8:9:9:11:11:12:13) sts.
With RS facing rejoin correct yarn, cast off
centre 13(13:15:15:17:19:21:23:25) sts and
work to end.
Complete to match first side rev shaping.

LEFT FRONT

Cast on 30(33:36:39:42:45:48:51:55) sts
using 3¹/₄mm (US 3) needles and yarn C.
Girls jacket
Work 5(5:5:5:5:5:7:7:7) rows in **moss st**.
Boys jacket
Work 2(2:2:2:2:2:4:4:4) rows in **moss st**.
Next row (buttonhole row)(RS): Work in
moss st to last 5 sts, K2tog, yrn needle twice,
K2tog, K1.
Next row: Moss st to end working into back
of loops made on previous row.
Work 1 row in **moss st**.
Both girls and boys jacket
Row 6(6:6:6:6:6:8:8:8) (WS): Work 5 sts in
Moss st, leave these sts on a holder, patt to
end. (25(28:31:34:37:40:43:46:50)sts)
Change to 4mm (US 6) needles and work 4
rows in st st beg with a K row and ending
with a WS row.
Inc 1 st at beg next row and
3(3:3:3:3:3:3:4:4:4) foll 10th rows.
(29(32:35:38:41:44:48:51:55)sts)
Cont without shaping until
9(9:9:9:9:11:11:11:13:13) rows shorter than
back to shoulder ending with a RS row.
Shape front neck
Cast off 3(3:3:3:3:4:4:4:4) sts at beg next row
and foll alt row.
Dec 1 st at neck edge on next
4(4:5:5:6:5:7:7:8) rows.
(19(22:24:27:29:31:33:36:39)sts)
Cont without further shaping until front
matches back to shoulder shaping ending
with a WS row.
Shape shoulder
Cast off 6(7:8:9:10:10:11:12:13) sts at beg
next row and foll alt row.
Work 1 row.
Cast off rem 7(8:8:9:9:11:11:12:13) sts.

RIGHT FRONT

Cast on 30(33:36:39:42:45:48:51:55) sts
using 3¹/₄mm (US 3) needles and yarn C.
Girls jacket
Work 2(2:2:2:2:2:4:4:4) rows in **moss st**.
Next row (buttonhole row) (RS): Patt 1,
K2tog, yrn twice, K2tog, patt to end.
Next row: Moss st to end working into back
of loops made on previous row.
Work 1 row in **moss st**.
Boys jacket
Work 5(5:5:5:5:5:7:7:7) rows in **moss st**.
Both girls and boys jacket
Row 6(6:6:6:6:6:8:8:8)(WS): Work in moss
st to last 5 sts, turn leaving rem sts on a
holder. (25(28:31:34:37:40:43:46:50)sts)
Change to 4mm (US 6) needles and complete
as given for left front, reversing all shaping.

SLEEVES (both alike)

Cast on 29(29:33:33:37:37:43:43:43) sts
using 3¹/₄mm (US 3) needles and yarn A.
Work 6(6:6:6:6:6:8:8:8) rows in **moss st** as

given for back.
Change to 4mm (US 6) needles and cont in st
st beg with a K row working in the colour
sequence as given for back and AT THE
SAME TIME shape sides as folls by inc 1 st at
each end of 3rd row and every foll 4th row
to 51(53:59:65:73:77:83:87:93) sts.
Cont without further shaping until sleeve
measures
19(20:23:25:28:30.5:35.5:38:40.5)cm or
length required from cast on edge ending
with a WS row.
Cast off loosely and evenly.

MAKING UP

PRESS all pieces as described on the
information page.
Join both shoulder seams using back stitch.
Button band (right front boys, left front girls)
Using 3¹/₄mm (US 3) needles slip sts from
holder onto LH needle, join in yarn C and
keeping patt correct cont in **moss st** until
band fits up front to neck shaping when
slightly stretched. Slip stitch into place.
Cast off.
Mark position of 6(6:6:6:7:7:7:8:8) buttons
the first to match buttonhole in band of
opposite front the last to come 1.5cm from
neck edge and remaining spaced evenly
between.
Buttonhole band
Work as for button hand with the addition of
buttonholes 5(5:5:5:6:6:6:7:7) worked as
before to correspond with markers.
Collar
Cast on 59(59:61:61:67:69:71:77:79) sts
using 3¹/₄mm (US 3) needles and yarn C.
Row 1(RS): K2, **moss st** to last 2 sts, K2.
Row 2: Rep first row again.
Next row (inc): K2, M1, **moss st** to last 2
sts, M1, K2.
Cont as set, inc as before on every foll 3rd
row until collar measures
6(6:7:7:8:8:9:9:10)cm from cast on edge.
Cast off in patt.
Patch pockets
Cast on 17(17:19:19:21:23:23:25:25) sts
using 3¹/₄mm (US 3) needles and yarn C.
Work in **moss st** until work measures
7.5(8:8.5:9:9.5:10:11:12:13)cm from cast on
edge ending with a WS row.
Dec 1 st at each end of next
4(4:4:4:5:5:5:6:6) rows.
(9(9:11:11:11:13:13:13:13)sts)
Cast off in **moss stitch**.
Sew pockets neatly into place.
Sew cast on edge of collar neatly into place
starting and ending halfway across front
bands and matching centre of collar with
centre back neck.
See information page for finishing
instructions leaving **moss st** border at bottom
side edges open to form tiny side vents.
Press all seams.

Fire Cracker

by KIM HARGREAVES

YARN
Rowan Chunky Tweed
Sweater
3(4:5:5:6:6:7:8:9) 100gm
(Photographed in Sandstone 882)
Jacket 7th(8th:9th) sizes only
(Photographed in Polar 879)
9(10:11) 100gm
Sizes
1st(2nd:3rd:4th:5th:6th:**7th:8th:9th**)
To fit
Actual width
29(32:35:38:41:44:**47:51:55**)cm
[11$\frac{1}{2}$(12$\frac{1}{2}$:13$\frac{3}{4}$:15:16:17$\frac{1}{4}$:**18$\frac{1}{2}$:20:21$\frac{1}{2}$**)ins]
Length
30.5(33:38:42:45:49.5:**53.5:57:61**)cm
[12:13:15:16$\frac{1}{2}$:18:19$\frac{1}{2}$:**21:22$\frac{1}{2}$:24**)ins]
Sleeve seam
15.5(18:19.5:21.5:22.5:25:**30.5:31.5:35**)cm
[6(7:7$\frac{3}{4}$:8$\frac{1}{2}$:9:10:**12:12$\frac{1}{2}$:13$\frac{3}{4}$**)ins]

NEEDLES
1 pair 5mm (no 6) (US 8) needles
1 pair 6mm (no 4) (US 10) needles

BUTTONS (jacket only) 3

TENSION
12 sts and 26 rows measured over fishermans rib using 6mm (US 10) needles (stretch rib slightly across width when measuring)

Special abbreviations
M2 = Make 2 sts - pick up loop before next st, knit and purl into back of loop: **tsb** = through stitch below:

Pattern note: The pattern for the jacket is for the largest 3 sizes only shown in **bold**.

Sweater
BACK
Cast on 35(39:43:47:51:55:**59:63:67**) sts using 6mm (US 10) needles.
Foundation row: Purl.
Row 1 (RS): K1, (K1tsb, P1) rep to last 2 sts, K1tsb, K1.
Row 2: K1, (P1, K1tsb), rep to last 2 sts, P1, K1.
These 2 rows form the pattern and are repeated throughout.
Cont in patt until work measures 18.5(20:23:26:25:27.5:30:**33:35.5:37**)cm from cast on edge ending with a WS row.
Shape raglan
Cast off 2(2:2:2:2:4:**4:4:4**) sts at beg next 2 rows.
Work 5(3:5:3:3:5:**5:5:5**) rows.
Next row (dec) (RS): K1, K1tsb, P3tog patt to last 5 sts, P3tog K1tsb, K1.
Work 5(3:5:3:3:5:**5:5:5**) rows.
2nd and 5th sizes only
Rep the last 4 rows once more.
All sizes
Dec 2 st at each end of next row, as before, and every foll 6th row to 11(11:15:15:15:15:**19:19:19**) sts ending with a WS row.

Work 3 rows.
Leave rem sts on a holder.

FRONT
Work as for back until 19(19:23:23:23:23:**27:27:27**) sts rem ending with a RS row.
Work 5 rows.
Next row (dec)(RS): K1, K1tsb, P3tog, patt until 11(11:15:15:15:15:**19:19:19**) sts rem, turn leaving rem sts on a holder.
Work each side of neck separately.
Keeping patt correct dec 1 st at neck edge on next 5 rows. (1st)
Fasten off.
With RS facing slip centre 3(3:7:7:7:7:**11:11:11**) sts onto a holder, rejoin yarn to rem sts, patt to last 5 sts, P3tog, K1tsb, K1.
Complete to match first side.

RIGHT SLEEVE
Cast on 23(23:27:27:31:31:**35:35:35**) sts using 5mm (US 8) needles.
Row 1 (RS): K1, (K1, P1) to last 2 sts, K2.
Row 2: K1, (P1, K1) to end.
Rep these 2 rows until work measures 4(4:4:5:5:5:**6:6:6**)cm from cast on edge ending with a WS row.
Change to 6mm (US 10) needles.
Row 1 (RS): K1, (K1tsb, P1) rep to last 2 sts, K1tsb, K1.
Row 2: K1, (P1, K1tsb), rep to last 2 sts, P1, K1.
These 2 rows form the pattern.
Keeping patt correct inc 1 st at each end of next row and every foll 8th(8th:10th:6th:6th:6th:**8th:8th:6th**) row to 31(31:35:39:43:47:**51:51:55**) sts.
Cont without further shaping until sleeve measures 15.5(18:19.5:21.5:22.5:25:**30.5:31.5:35**)cm from cast on edge ending with a WS row.
* Shape raglans
Cast off 2(2:2:2:2:4:**4:4:4**) sts at beg next 2 rows.
Work 2(4:2:2:2:2:**2:6:2**) rows.
Next row (dec) (RS): K1, K1tsb, P3tog patt to last 5 sts, P3tog K1tsb, K1.
Work 5(5:5:3:3:5:**3:5:5**)
4th, 5th and 7th sizes only
Rep the last 4 rows once more.
All sizes
Dec 2 st at each end of next row, as before, and every foll 6th row to 11 sts ending with a WS row.
Work 5 rows. ******
Shape sleeve top
Next row (RS): Cast off 4 sts, work to last 5 sts, P3tog, K1tsb, K1.
Dec 1 st at end of next row and on the same edge on foll 2 rows.
Cast off rem 2 sts.

LEFT SLEEVE
Work as for right sleeve to **.
Shape sleeve top
Next row (RS): K1, K1tsb, P3tog, patt to

end.
Cast off 5 sts, patt to end.
Dec 1 st at end of next row and on the same edge foll row.
Cast off rem 2 sts.

Jacket
BACK
Following three largest sizes only, work as for sweater back.

POCKET LININGS (make 2)
Cast on 15 sts using 6mm (US 10) needles.
Work 22 rows in st st beg with a K row.
Leave sts on a holder.

LEFT FRONT
Cast on **35(37:39)** sts using using 6mm (US 10) needles.
Foundation row: Purl.
Row 1 (RS): K1, (K1tsb, P1) rep to last 2 sts, K1tsb, K1.
Row 2: K1, (P1, K1tsb), rep to last 2 sts, P1, K1.
These 2 rows form the pattern and are repeated throughout.
Cont in patt until work measures **15(16:17)**cm from cast on edge ending with a WS row.
Place pocket
Patt **7(8:9)**, slip next 15 sts onto a holder, patt across first sts of first pocket lining, patt to end.
Cont in patt until work is 4 rows shorter than back to armhole shaping ending with a WS row.
Divide for collar
Next row (RS): Patt to last 7 sts, turn leaving rem 7 sts on a holder for collar.
Work 3 rows.
Shape raglan and front neck
1st size only
Cast off 4 sts at beg next row, patt to last 2 sts, K2tog.
Cont dec at armhole edge on the following 8th row and then every foll 6th row as given for back and AT THE SAME TIME dec 1 st at neck edge on every foll 6th row until 1 st remains.
Fasten off.
2nd and 3rd size only
Cast off 4 sts at beg next row, patt to end.
Work 1 row.
Cont dec at armhole edge on foll 3rd row and then every foll 6th row as given for back and at the same time dec 1 st at neck edge on next row and 8(5) foll 6th rows and then for larger size 3 foll 8th rows. (1st)
Fasten off.
Mark position of 3 buttons, the first to come 2cm below sts on holder for collar, the 3rd opposite top of pocket and other spaced evenly between.

RIGHT FRONT
Work as given for left front reversing placing of pocket and all shaping and with the addition of 3 buttonholes worked to

correspond with markers as folls:
Buttonhole row (RS): Patt 3, yon, K2tog, patt to end.

RIGHT SLEEVE
Cast on 35 sts using 6mm (US 10) needles.
Foundation row: Purl.
Row 1 (RS): K1, (K1tsb, P1) rep to last 2 sts, K1tsb, K1.
Row 2: K1, (P1, K1tsb), rep to last 2 sts, P1, K1.
These 2 rows form the pattern.
Cont in patt until work measures 12cm from cast on edge, to form turnback cuff, ending with a WS row.
Keeping patt correct inc 1 st at each end of next row and every foll 6th row to 51(51:55) sts.
Cont without further shaping until sleeve measures 36.5(37.5:41)cm from cast on edge ending with a WS row. **
Complete as for right sleeve of sweater working from *.

LEFT SLEEVE
Work as for right sleeve to ** then complete as for left sweater sleeve.

MAKING UP
Steam pieces with a steam iron.
Sweater
Join sleeves to front using a flat stitch.
Join right sleeve to back.
Leave left back seam open.
Neckband
With RS facing and using 5mm (US 8) needles, pick up and K 8 sts across top of left sleeve, 6 sts down left front neck, keeping patt correct work in K1, P1 rib across 3(3:7:7:7:7:11:11:11) from holder st centre front, pick up and knit 6 sts up right front neck and 7 sts across top of right sleeve neck, rib across 11(11:15:15:15:15:19:19:19) sts at back neck.
(41(41:49:49:49:49:57:57:57)sts)
Row 1 (WS): (K1, P1) to last st, K1.
Row 2: (P1, K1) to last st, P1.
Rep these 2 rows 1(1:1:1:2:2:2:2:2) times more.
Cast off **very** loosely in rib.
Jacket
Join all raglan seams using a flat seam.
Collar
Left side
With RS facing and using 6mm (US 10)

needles slip 7 sts from holder onto LH needle.
Next row (RS)(inc): K1, K1tsb, M2, patt to end. (9sts)
Work 7 rows.
Rep these last 8 rows 4 times more then inc once more ending at outside edge. (19sts)
Next row (WS): Cast off 7 sts, return st on RH needle to LH needle, recast on 7 sts using cable method (ie. insert RH needle between first 2 sts on LH needle, yon, place loop onto LH needle).
Cont without further shaping until collar fits up front, across top of sleeve and across to centre back, ending at the inside edge.
Cast off 6 sts at beg next row and foll alt row.
Work 1 row.
Cast off rem 7 sts.
Right side
Work as for left side reversing all shaping.
Pocket tops (both alike)
With RS facing slip sts from holder on a 5mm (US 8) needle and work 2 rows in patt.
Cast off in patt.
See information page for finishing instructions.

Lazy Daisy Sweater
by KIM HARGREAVES

YARNS
Rowan Handknit D.K. Cotton

A	Summer Pud.	243	8(9:10:11:13)	50gm
B	Tomato	236	1(1:1:1:1)	50gm
C	Popcorn	229	1(1:1:1:1)	50gm
D	Boston Fern	230	1(1:1:1:1)	50gm
E	Jade	235	1(1:1:1:2)	50gm
F	Diana	287	1(1:1:1:2)	50gm
G	Royal	294	1(1:1:1:1)	50gm

Sizes
1st(2nd:3rd:4th:5th)
To fit
3-4(4-6:6-8:8-9:9-10) yrs
Actual width
41(43.5:47:51:54.5)cm
[16(17:18^1/2:20:21^1/2)ins]
Length
45.5(48:52:55.5:58)cm
[18(19:20^1/2:22:23)ins]
Sleeve length
28(30.5:35.5:38:40.5)cm
[11(12:14:15:16)ins]

NEEDLES
1 pair 3^1/4mm (no 10) (US 3) needles
1 pair 4mm (no 8) (US 6) needles

TENSION
22 sts and 28 rows to 10cm measured over patterned stocking stitch using 4mm (US 6) needles

BACK
Cast on 90(96:104:112:120) sts using 3^1/4mm (US 3) needles and yarn A.
Work 2.5cm in K2, P2 rib ending with a WS row.

Change to 4mm (US 6) needles, joining in and breaking off colours as required and using the **intarsia** technique described on the information page cont in patt from chart for back until chart row 120(128:138:148:156) completed ending with a WS row.
Shape shoulders and back neck
Cast off 9(10:11:12:13) sts at beg of next 2 rows.
Cast off 9(10:11:12:13), K14(15:16:17:18) sts, turn leaving rem sts on a holder.
Work each side of neck separately.
Cast off 4 sts, work to end.
Cast off rem 10(11:12:13:14) sts.
With RS facing rejoin appropriate yarns to rem sts, cast off centre 26(26:28:30:32) sts, work to end.
Complete to match first side.

FRONT
Work as for back until chart row 112(120:128:138:144) completed ending with a WS row.
Shape front neck
Patt 38(41:45:49:53) sts, turn leaving rem sts on a holder.
Work each side of neck separately.
Cast off 3 sts at beg next row and foll alt row.
Dec 1 st at neck edge on next 4(4:5:6:7) rows. (28(31:34:37:40)sts)
Cont without further shaping until front matches back to shoulder shaping ending with a WS row.
Shape shoulder
Cast off 9(10:11:12:13) sts at beg next row and foll alt row.
Work 1 row.

Cast off rem 10(11:12:13:14) sts.
With RS facing join appropriate yarns to rem sts, cast off centre 14 sts, work to end.
Complete as for first side reversing shaping.

SLEEVES (both alike)
Cast on 40(40:44:44:50) sts using 3^1/4mm (US 3) needles and yarn A.
Work 2.5cm in K2, P2 rib ending with a WS row.
Change to 4mm (US 6) needles and working between appropriate markers, cont in patt from chart until chart row 72(78:92:100:106) completed and AT THE SAME TIME shape sides by inc 1 st at each end of 3rd row and every foll 3rd row to 74(74:74:74:76) sts and then every foll 4th row to 80(84:90:94:102) sts and ending with a WS row.
Cast off loosely and evenly.

MAKING UP
PRESS all pieces as described on the information page.
Join right shoulder seam using back stitch.
Neck band
With RS facing, using 3^1/4mm (US 3) needles and yarn A, beg at left shoulder, pick up and knit 15(15:17:17:19) sts down left front neck, 14 sts across centre front, pick up and knit 15(15:17:17:19) sts up right front neck, and 34(34:36:38:40) across back neck.
(78(78:84:86:92)sts)
Work 2cm in K2, P2 rib.
Cast off evenly in rib.
Join left shoulder seam using back stitch and neck band using edge to edge stitch.
See information page for finishing instructions.

KEY
A □
B ⊞
C ▨
D ⊠
E ⊡
F ▲
G ⊙

156
150
140
130
120
110
100
90
80
70
60
50
40
30
20
10

1st size
2nd size
3rd size
4th size
5th size

1st & 2nd size sleeve
3rd & 4th size sleeve
5th size sleeve

1st size
2nd size
3rd size
4th size
5th size

Checker

by LOUISA HARDING

YARNS
Rowan Den-m-nit
6(7:9:10:10:11:13:15:15) 50gm

Sizes
1st(2nd:3rd:4th:5th:6th:7th:8th:9th)
To fit
6mth(9mth:1-2:2-3:3-4:4-6:6-8:8-9:9-10) yrs
Actual width
29(32:35:38:41:44:47:51:55)cm
[11½(12½:13½:15:16½:17½:18½:20:21½)
ins]
Length after washing
30.5(33:38:42:45:49.5:53.5:57:61)cm
[12(13:15:16½:18:19½:21:22½:24)ins]
Sleeve length after washing
19(20:23:25:28:30.5:35.5:38:40.5)cm
[7½(8:9:10:11:12:14:15:16)ins]

NEEDLES
1 pair 3¼mm (no 10) (US 3) needles
1 pair 4mm (no 8) (US 6) needles

BUTTONS 4(4:5:5:5:5:5:6:6)

TENSION BEFORE WASHING
20 sts and 28 rows to 10 cm measured over
stocking stitch using 4mm (US 6) needles

BACK
Cast on 58(64:70:76:82:88:94:102:110) sts
using 3¼mm (US 3) needles.
Working between markers for appropriate
size work 10 rows in pattern from the chart
for back.
Change to 4mm (US 6) needles and cont in
patt from chart repeating the 32 row patt as
indicated throughout until work measures
33.5(36.5:42:46.5:50:55.5:60:64.5:68.5)cm
from cast on edge ending with a WS row
(this allows for shrinkage after washed).

Shape back neck
Next row (RS): Patt
21(23:25:27:29:32:34:37:41) sts, turn leaving
rem sts on a holder.
Work each side of neck separately.
Dec 1 st at neck edge on next 3 rows, ending
at side edge.(18(20:22:24:26:29:31:34:38)sts)
Leave rem sts on a holder.
With RS facing rejoin yarn to rem sts, cast off
centre 16(18:20:22:24:24:26:28:28) sts, patt
to end. Complete to match first side.

POCKET LININGS (work 2)
Cast on 20(20:20:22:22:22:24:24:24) sts
using 4mm (US 6) needles.
Work 22(24:26:28:30:30:32:34:34) rows in
st st beg with a K row. Leave sts on a holder.

LEFT FRONT
Cast on 34(37:40:43:46:49:52:56:60) sts
using 3¼mm (US 3).
Working between markers for appropriate
size of left front, work 9 rows in patt from
chart.
Chart row 10 (WS): Patt 5 sts, leave these
on a holder, patt to end.
(29(32:35:38:41:44:47:51:55)sts)
Change to 4mm (US 6) needles and cont in
patt from chart for left front until
34(36:38:40:42:42:44:46:46) rows in all
completed ending with a WS row.
Place pocket
Next row (RS): Patt 4(6:8:8:10:10:10:12:14)
sts, slip next 20(20:20:22:22:22:24:24:24) sts
onto a holder and knit across
20(20:20:22:22:22:24:24:24) sts from pocket
lining, patt to end.
Cont in patt until front is
11(11:13:15:17:17:17:19:19) shorter than
back to **shape back neck** ending with a RS
row.

Shape front neck
Cast off 5(5:5:6:6:6:6:6:6) sts at beg next
row, patt to end.
Dec 1 st at neck edge on next
4(5:6:5:5:5:6:6:6) rows and
2(2:2:3:4:4:4:5:5) foll alt rows.
(18(20:22:24:26:29:31:34:38)sts)
Work without further shaping until front
matches back to shoulder ending with a WS
row. Leave sts on a holder.

RIGHT FRONT
Cast on 34(37:40:43:46:49:52:56:60) sts
using 3¼mm (US 3).
Working between markers for appropriate
size of right front, work 9 rows in patt from
chart.
Chart row 10 (WS): Patt to last 5 sts, turn
leaving rem 5 sts on a holder.
(29(32:35:38:41:44:47:51:55)sts)
Change to 4mm (US 6) needles and complete
as given for left front reversing placing of
pocket and all shaping.

SLEEVES (both alike)
Cast on 29(29:33:33:37:37:43:43:43) sts
using 3¼mm (US 3) needles. Work 10 rows
in pattern from chart for sleeve.
Change to 4mm (US 6) needles and cont in
patt from chart rep the 16 row patt as
indicated throughout and inc 1 st at each end
of 3rd row and every foll 4th row to
51(53:59:65:73:77:71:71:81) sts and then for
3 largest sizes only every foll 6th row to
83(87:93) sts, take extra sts into pattern as
they occur. (51(53:59:65:73:77:83:87:93)sts)
Cont without shaping until sleeve measures
22(23:26.5:28.5:32:35:41:43.5:46.5) cm
from cast on edge ending with a WS row
(this allows for shrinkage after washed).
Cast off loosely and evenly.

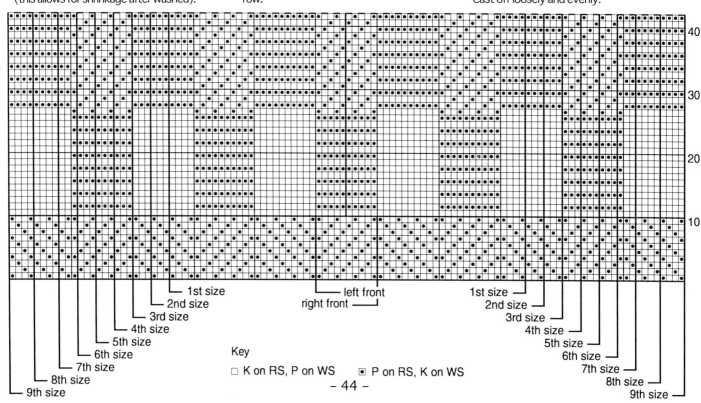

40

30

20

10

1st size
2nd size
3rd size
4th size
5th size
6th size
7th size
8th size
9th size

left front
right front

1st size
2nd size
3rd size
4th size
5th size
6th size
7th size
8th size
9th size

Key

□ K on RS, P on WS   ▣ P on RS, K on WS

MAKING UP

PRESS all pieces as described on the information page.

Button band

With WS of right front facing for boy, RS of left front facing for girl and using 3¼mm (US 3) needles, slip 5 sts from holder onto lefthand needle, rejoin yarn and patt across row in diagonal patt as set, and AT THE SAME TIME inc 1 st at **inside** edge of front band. (6 sts).
Cont in diagonal patt until band fits up front to beg of neck shaping ending with a WS row, slip st into place. Cast off.
Mark position of 4(4:5:5:5:5:6:6) buttons the first to come at top of border, the last to come 1.5cm down from neck shaping and others spaced evenly between.

Buttonhole band

With RS of left front facing for boy and WS of right front facing for girl and using 3¼mm (US 3) needles slip sts from holder onto lefthand needle. Keeping patt correct and inc 1 st at inside edge work as for buttonband with the addition of 4(4:5:5:5:5:6:6)

buttonholes to correspond with markers as follows:
Buttonhole row (RS): Patt 2, yon twice, k2tog, patt 2.
Next row: Patt to end dropping one of the loops.

Pocket Edgings

With RS facing and using 3¼mm (US 3) needles slip sts from holder onto LH needle. Knit 3 rows. Cast off knitwise.

Collar

Using 3¼mm (US 3) needles cast on 55(57:61:67:75:75:77:83:83) sts.
Knit 10 rows.
Next row: K2, M1, Knit to last 2 sts, M1, K2.
Knit 3 rows.
Rep these last 4 rows until collar measures 7(7:7:8:8:8:9:10:10)cm from cast on edge.
Cast off loosely and evenly knitwise.
Join both shoulder seams by casting off sts together on the RS.

Machine wash all pieces as given on ball band before sewing together.

See information page for finishing instructions.

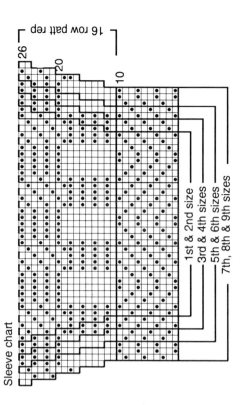

Sleeve chart

Sea Shanty
by LOUISA HARDING

YARN

Den-m-nit
6(7:8:8:10:12:14:14:16) 50gm

Sizes

1st(2nd:3rd:4th:5th:6th:7th:8th:9th)
To fit
6mth(9mth:1-2:2-3:3-4:4-6:6-8:8-9:9-10) yrs
Actual width
28.5(31.5:34.5:37.5:40.5:43.5:46.5:50.5:54.5)cm
[11¼(12:13½:14¾:16:17:18¼:20:21½)ins]
Length after washing
30.5(33:38:42:45:49.5:53.5:57:61)cm
[12(13:15:16½:18:19½:21:22½:24)ins]
Sleeve length after washing
19(20:23:25:28:30.5:35.5:38:40.5)cm
[7½(8:9:10:11:12:14:15:16)ins]

NEEDLES

1 pair 3¼mm (no 10) (US 3) needles
1 pair 4mm (no 8) (US 6) needles
Cable needle

BUTTONS

1st, 2nd, 3rd & 4th sizes only - 4

TENSION

20 sts and 28 rows to 10 cm measured over pattern using 4mm (US 6) needles before washing

Special Abbreviations

T4BR = Twist 4 back right - slip next st onto CN, hold at back, K1tbl, P1, K1tbl from LH needle, then P1, from CN
T4FL = Twist 4 front left - slip next 3 sts onto CN, and hold at front, P1 from LH needle, then K1tbl, P1, K1tbl from CN
T7L = Twist 7 left - slip next 3 sts onto CN, hold at front, (K1tbl, P1) twice from LH needle, then P1, K1tbl from CN

CABLE PATTERN (worked over 11 sts)
Row 1 (RS): (P1, K1tbl) twice, P3, (K1tbl, P1) twice
Row 2: (K1, P1tbl) twice, K3, (P1tbl, K1) twice
Row 3: Work as row 1.
Row 4: Work as row 2.
Row 5: P1, T4FL, P1, T4BR, P1
Row 6: K2, (P1tbl, K1) 4 times, K1
Row 7: P2, T7L, P2.
Row 8: Work as row 6.
Row 9: P1, T4BR, P1, T4FL P1
Row 10: Work as row 2.
Rows 3 - 10 form the 8 row pattern repeat.

BACK

Cast on 57(63:69:75:81:87:93:101:109) using 3¼mm (US 3) needles.
Work 10 rows from chart, beg and ending where indicated for appropriate size and work the 28 st patt 2(2:2:2:2:3:3:3:3) times across row.
Change to 4mm (US 6) needles and cont until chart row 34 completed.
Cont in patt rep the 32 row patt as indicated on chart until work measures 33.5(36.5:42:46.5:50:55:59:63:68)cm from cast on edge ending with a WS row (this allows for shrinkage after washing).
Shape shoulder and back neck
Patt 20(22:24:26:28:31:33:36:40) turn, leave rem sts on a holder.
Work each side of neck separately.
Cast off 3 sts, patt to end. (17(19:21:23:25:28:30:33:37)sts)
Leave sts on a holder.
5th, 6th, 7th, 8th & 9th sizes only
Slip centre 25(25:27:29:29) sts onto a holder, rejoin yarn and patt to end.
Complete to match first side.
1st, 2nd, 3rd and 4th sizes only

Slip centre 17(19:21:23) sts onto a holder, rejoin yarn and patt to end.
Work 1 row.
Work button band
Next row (RS): Cast off 3 sts, (K2tbl, P2) to last 1(3:1:3) sts, K1(2:1:2) tbl, P0(1:0:1). (17(19:21:23)sts)
Next row: K0(1:0:1), P1(2:1:2) tbl, (K2, P2tbl) to end.
Work 2 more rows in rib as set. Cast off

FRONT

Work as for back until work is 12(14:14:16:16:18:18:20:20) rows shorter than back to **shape shoulder and back neck.**
Shape front neck and shoulder
Patt 24(26:28:31:33:36:38:41:45) sts, turn, leave rem sts on a holder.
Work each side of neck separately.
Dec 1 st at neck edge on next 4 rows and 3(3:3:4:4:4:4:4:4) foll alt rows. (17(19:21:23:25:28:30:33:37)sts)
Work without further shaping until front matches back to shoulder shaping ending with a WS row. *
5th, 6th, 7th, 8th and 9th sizes only
Leave sts on a holder.
1st, 2nd, 3rd and 4th sizes
Work buttonhole band
Next row (RS): (K2tbl, P2) to last 1(3:1:3) sts, K1(2:1:2) tbl, P0(1:0:1).
Next row (buttonhole row): Keeping rib patt correct, rib 1(3:5:7), (rib 2tog, yon, rib 6) twice.
Work 2 more rows in rib as set. Cast off
All sizes
Slip centre 9(11:13:13:15:15:17:19:19) sts onto a holder, rejoin yarn to rem sts, patt to end.
Complete to match first side to *
Leave sts on a holder.

SLEEVES (both alike)

Cast on 31(31:35:35:39:39:45:45:45) sts using 3¼mm (US 3) needles.
Work 10 rows in patt from chart working between markers for appropriate size. Change to 4mm (US 6) needles and cont in patt from chart and AT THE SAME TIME inc 1 st at each end of next row and every foll 4th row to 51(53:59:65:73:77:71:71:81) sts and then for 3 largest sizes only every foll 6th row to 83(87:93) sts, taking the extra stitches into textured patt as set.
(51:53:59:65:73:77:83:87:93)sts)
Cont without further shaping until sleeve measures 21(22:26:28:31:33.5:39:42:46)cm from cast on edge ending with a WS row (this allows for shrinkage after washing). Cast off evenly in patt.

MAKING UP

Join left shoulder seam by casting off sts together on RS.

Neckband

With RS facing, using 3¼mm (US 3) needles and beg at left shoulder, **on first 4 sizes only**, pick up and K 3 sts across buttonhole band, 12(14:14:16:16:16:17:20:20), down left front, work across sts
9(11:13:13:15:15:17:19:19) from holder at centre, pick up and K
12(14:14:16:17:17:19:21:21) sts up right front neck and 3(3:3:3:4:4:4:4:4) sts down back neck, work across sts
17(19:21:23:25:25:27:29:29) from holder at centre back, pick up and K 3(3:3:3:3:3:4:3:3) sts up back neck and on **first 4 sizes only** pick up and knit 3 sts across button band.
(62:70:74:80:80:80:88:96:96)sts)

1st, 2nd & 3rd sizes only

Row 1 (WS): P2tbl, (K2, P2tbl) to end.
Row 2 (RS)(buttonhole): K2tbl, yon, P2tog, (K2tbl, P2) to last 0(2:0) sts, K0(2:0)tbl.
Work 7 more rows in rib as set, working buttonhole on 4th row as before and ending with a WS row. Cast off in rib.

4th size only

Row 1 (WS): (K2, P2tbl) 3 times, keeping patt correct work 11 sts in cable patt, (P2tbl, K2) 6 times, p2tbl, work 11 sts in cable patt, (P2tbl, K2) 5 times.
Row 2 (RS)(buttonhole): P2, yon, K2tog, (P2, K2tbl) 4 times, work 11 sts in cable patt, (K2tbl, P2) 6 times, K2tbl, work 11 sts in cable patt, (K2tbl, P2) to end.

Work 7 more rows in rib as set, working buttonhole on 4th row as before and ending with a WS row. Cast off in rib.

5th, 6th, 7th, 8th & 9th sizes only

Row 1: (WS): P2(2:0:0:0)tbl, (K2, P2tbl) 2(2:3:3:3) times, work 11 sts in cable patt, (P2tbl, K2) 7(7:8:9:9) times, P2tbl, work 11 sts in cable patt, (P2tbl, K2) 4(4:5:6:6) times, P2(2:0:0:0)tbl.
Row 2: K2(2:0:0:0)tbl, (P2, K2tbl) 4(4:5:6:6) times, work 11 sts in cable patt, (K2tbl, P2) 7(7:8:9:9) times, K2tbl, work 11 sts in cable patt, (K2tbl, P2) 2(2:3:3:3) times, K2(2:0:0:0)tbl.

Rep these 2 rows until neckband measures 4(4:5:6:6)cm ending with a WS row. Cast off in rib.
Wash all pieces, as described on the ball band, before sewing together.
See information page for finishing instructions.

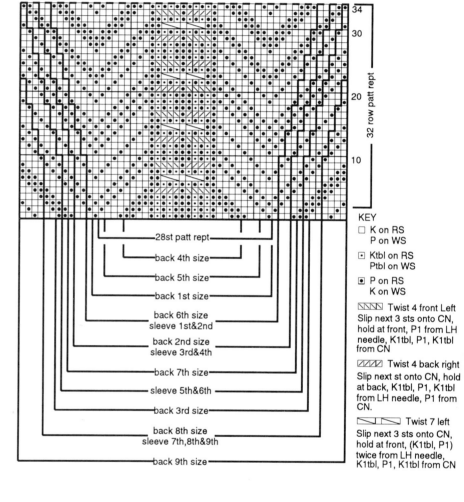

- 28st patt rept -
- back 4th size -
- back 5th size -
- back 1st size -
- back 6th size / sleeve 1st&2nd -
- back 2nd size / sleeve 3rd&4th -
- back 7th size -
- sleeve 5th&6th -
- back 3rd size -
- back 8th size / sleeve 7th,8th&9th -
- back 9th size -

32 row patt rept

KEY

□ K on RS / P on WS

⊡ Ktbl on RS / Ptbl on WS

◉ P on RS / K on WS

⧄⧄⧄⧄ Twist 4 front Left
Slip next 3 sts onto CN, hold at front, P1 from LH needle, K1tbl, P1, K1tbl from CN

⧅⧅⧅⧅ Twist 4 back right
Slip next st onto CN, hold at back, K1tbl, P1, K1tbl from LH needle, P1 from CN.

⧄⧄⧄ Twist 7 left
Slip next 3 sts onto CN, hold at front, (K1tbl, P1) twice from LH needle, K1tbl, P1, K1tbl from CN

Queen of Hearts

by KIM HARGREAVES

YARNS

Rowan Handknit D.K. Cotton
5(6:7:9:11:13:15) 50gm
(1st size photographed in Gerba 223, 4th size in Raspberry 240)

Sizes

1st(2nd:3rd:4th:5th:6th:7th)

To fit
6mth(1:2-3:4-5:5-6:7-7-8:9-10) yrs

Actual width
29(34:37.5:42.5:46:51:55)cm
[11½(13½:14¾:16¾:18:20:21½)ins]

Length

30.5(37.5:42:47:51.5:57:61)cm
[12(14¾:16½:18½:20¼:22½:24)ins]

Sleeve length
19(21.5:25:29:33.5:38:40.5)cm
[7½(8½:9½:11½:13:15:16)ins)]

NEEDLES

1 pair 3¼mm (no 10) (US 3) needles
1 pair 4mm (no 8) (US 6) needles

Buttons (1st, 2nd, 3rd and 4th sizes only) - 3

TENSION

21 sts and 31 rows to 10cm measured over patterned stocking stitch using 4mm (US 6) needles

BACK

Cast on 61(71:79:89:97:107:115) sts using 3¼mm (US 3) needles.
Work in **moss stitch** as folls:
Row 1 (RS): K1, (P1, K1) to end.
Rep this row 5(5:5:5:7:7:7) times more ending with a WS row.

Change to 4mm (US 6) needles.
1st, 3rd, 5th & 7th sizes only
Work 24 rows in patt from appropriate chart starting and ending as indicated and rep the 18 st patt rep 3(4:5:6) times across row.
2nd, 4th & 6th sizes only
Work 48 rows in patt from appropriate chart starting and ending as indicated and rep the 18 st patt rep 3(4:5) times across row. *
All sizes
Cont rep the 24 row patt until work measures 25.5(32.5:37:42:51.5:57:61)cm from cast on edge ending with a WS row.
1st, 2nd, 3rd & 4th sizes only
Divide for back neck
Next row (RS): Patt 30(35:39:44) sts, turn leaving rem sts on a holder, work each side of neck separately.
Patt note: To give the back opening a neat edge always K the edge st on every row (RS or WS row)
Cont without shaping until work measures 30.5(37.5:42:47)cm from cast on edge ending with a WS row.
Shape shoulder
Cast off 6(7:8:9) sts at beg next row.
Cast off 7(8:9:11) sts, patt to end.
Cast off 6(8:9:10) sts, patt to end.
Cast off 4 sts, patt to end.
Cast off rem 7(8:9:10) sts.
With RS facing rejoin yarn to rem sts, K2tog, patt to end. (30(35:39:44)sts)
Complete to match first side rev all shaping.
5th, 6th & 7th sizes only
Shape shoulders and back neck
Cast off 10(12:13) sts at beg next 2 rows.
Cast off 11(12:13) sts, patt 15(16:18) sts, turn leaving rem sts on a holder.
Work each side of neck separately.
Cast off 4 sts, patt to end.
Cast off rem 11(12:14) sts.
With RS facing rejoin yarn to rem sts, cast off centre 25(27:27) sts, patt to end.
Complete as for first side rev all shaping.

FRONT
Work as for back to *.
All sizes
Cont rep the 24 row patt until front is 8(10:10:10:12:12:12) rows shorter then back to shoulder shaping ending with a WS row.
Shape front neck
Patt 25(30:34:37:41:46:50), turn leaving rem sts on a holder.
Work each side of neck separately.
Dec 1 st at neck edge on next 6(7:8:8:9:10:10) rows.
(19(23:26:29:32:36:40)sts)
Cont without further shaping until front matches back to shoulder shaping ending with a WS row.
Shape shoulder
Cast off 6(7:8:9:10:12:13) sts at beg next row and 6(8:9:10:11:12:13) sts at beg foll alt row.
Work 1 row.
Cast off rem 7(8:9:10:11:12:14) sts.
With RS facing rejoin yarn to rem sts, cast off centre 11(11:11:15:15:15:15) sts and patt to end.
Complete as for first side reversing shaping.

SLEEVES (both alike)
Cast on 31(35:35:39:43:47:47) sts using 3¼mm (US 3) needles.
Work in **moss st** as folls:

Row 1 (RS): P1, (K1, P1) to end.
Rep this row 5(5:5:5:7:7:7) times more ending with a WS row.
Change to 4mm (US 6) needles and work 24 rows in patt from chart for sleeve, inc each end of 3rd row and every foll 4th row.
Taking extra sts in patt, cont inc every 4th row to 53(59:67:77:87:85:85) sts and then for **6th and 7th size only** every foll 6th row to 91(95) sts. (53(59:67:77:87:91:95)sts)
Cont without further shaping until sleeve measures 19(21.5:25:29:33.5:38:40.5)cm or length required from cast on edge ending with a WS row. Cast off loosely and evenly.

MAKING UP
PRESS all pieces as described on the information page.
1st, 2nd, 3rd & 4th sizes only
Join both shoulder seams using back stitch.
Neck band
With RS facing, using 3¼mm (US 3) needles, beg at left back neck opening, pick up and knit 12(13:14:16) sts across back neck to

shoulder, 12(14:14:14) down left front neck, 11(11:11:15) sts across centre front, pick up and knit 12(14:14:14) sts up right front neck, and 12(13:14:16) across right back neck. (59(65:67:75)sts)
Work 4(4:5:5) rows in **moss st**.
Cast off evenly in pattern.
Mark position of 3 buttons down left back opening 1st to come in the neckband others spaced evenly.
Work button loops to correspond down right back opening.
5th, 6th & 7th sizes only
Join right shoulder seam using back stitch.
With RS facing, using 3¼mm (US 3) needles, pick up and knit 16 sts down left front neck, 15 sts across centre front 16 sts up right front neck and 33(35:35) sts across back neck. (80(82:82)sts)
Work 6 rows in **moss st**.
Cast off evenly in pattern.
See information page for finishing instructions leaving 5(5:6:6:8:8:8)cm open at side seam to form vents. Press all seams.

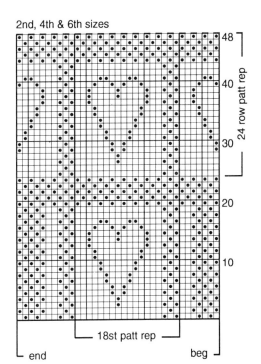

2nd, 4th & 6th sizes

Key
☐ K on RS, P on WS
▣ P on RS, K on WS

1st, 3rd, 5th & 7th sizes

18st patt rep

Sleeve chart all sizes

1st size
2nd & 3rd size
4th size
5th size
6th & 7th size

Odd Job

by KIM HARGREAVES

YARNS
Rowan Magpie Aran
A 2(3:3:4:4:5:5:6:7) 100gm
B 1(1:1:1:1:1:1:1:1) 100gm
Sweater
(Photographed in Nat 002 and Admiral 504)
Cardigan
(Photographed in Raven 62 and Dapple 450)

Sizes
1st(2nd:3rd:4th:5th:6th:7th:8th:9th)
To fit
6mth(9mth:1-2:2-3:3-4:4-6:6-8:8-9:9-10) yrs
Actual width
29.5(31.5:35:38:40.5:44:47:50.5:55)cm
[11$\frac{1}{2}$(12$\frac{1}{2}$:13$\frac{1}{2}$:15:16:17$\frac{1}{2}$:18$\frac{1}{2}$:20:21$\frac{1}{2}$)ins]
Length
30.5(33:38:42:45:49.5:53.5:57:61)cm
[12(13:15:16$\frac{1}{2}$:17$\frac{1}{2}$:19$\frac{1}{2}$:21:22$\frac{1}{2}$:24)ins]
Sleeve length
19(20:23:25:28:30.5:35.5:38:40.5)cm
[7$\frac{1}{2}$(8:9:10:11:12:14:15:16)ins]

NEEDLES
1 pair 4mm (no 8) (US 6) needles
1 pair 5mm (no 6) (US 8) needles

BUTTONS - 5

TENSION
18 sts and 23 rows to 10cm measured over
stocking stitch using 5mm (US 8) needles

Sweater
BACK
Cast on 52(56:62:68:72:78:84:90:98) sts
using 4mm (US 6) needles and yarn A and
work in **two colour rib** as folls:
Row 1 (RS): P0(0:2:0:0:2:0:2:2)A, (K2B,
P2A) to end.
Row 2: (K2A, P2B) to last 0(0:2:0:0:2:0:2:2)
sts, K0(0:2:0:0:2:0:2:2)A.
Rep these 2 rows twice more inc 1 st at end
of last row.
(53(57:63:69:73:79:85:91:99)sts)
Change to 5mm (US 8) needles.
* Working between markers for appropriate
size and using the **fairisle** technique as
described on the information page cont in
patt from chart until chart row 38 completed.
Using yarn A only cont in st st until work
measures
30.5(33:38:42:45:49.5:53.5:57:61)cm from
cast on edge ending with a WS row. **
Shape shoulders and back neck
Cast off 5(6:6:7:7:8:9:10:11) sts at beg next 2
rows.
Cast off 6(6:7:7:8:9:9:10:11) sts K
10(10:11:12:12:13:14:14:16), turn leaving
rem sts on a holder.
Work each side of neck separately.
Cast off 4 sts, patt to end.
Cast off rem 6(6:7:8:8:9:10:10:12)sts.
With RS facing slip centre
11(13:15:17:19:19:21:23:23)sts onto a
holder for back neck, rejoin yarn to rem sts,
patt to end.
Complete to match first side rev shaping.

FRONT
Work as for back until front is
10(10:10:12:12:12:12:14:14) rows shorter
than back to shoulder shaping ending with a
WS row.
Shape front neck
Knit 23(25:27:30:32:35:38:40:44), turn
leaving rem sts on a holder.
Work each side of neck separately.
Cast off 3 sts, P to end.
Dec 1 st at neck edge on next
3(4:4:5:5:5:5:5:5) rows and
0(0:0:0:1:1:2:2:2) alt rows.
(17(18:20:22:23:26:28:30:34)sts)
Cont without further shaping until front
matches back to shoulder shaping ending
with a WS row.
Shape shoulder
Cast off 5(6:6:7:7:8:9:10:11) sts, beg next row
and 6(6:7:7:8:9:9:10:11) sts beg foll alt row.
Work 1 row.
Cast off rem 6(6:7:8:8:9:10:10:12)sts.
With RS facing slip centre
7(7:9:9:9:9:9:11:11) sts onto a holder for
front neck, K to end.
Complete as for first side rev all shaping.

SLEEVES (both alike)
Cast on 24(24:28:28:32:32:38:38:38) sts
using 4mm (US 6) needles and yarn A.
Work 6 rows in **two colour rib** as folls:
Row 1 (RS): P0(0:0:0:0:0:2:2:2)A, (K2B,
P2A) to end.
Row 2: (K2A, P2B) to last 0(0:0:0:0:0:2:2:2)
sts, K0(0:0:0:0:0:2:2:2)A.
Rep these 2 rows twice more inc 1 st at end
of last row.
(25(25:29:29:33:33:39:39:39)sts)
* Change to 5mm (US 8) needles, working
between appropriate markers, work **12 rows**
in patt from chart and AT THE SAME TIME
shape sides by inc 1 st at each end of 3rd
row and 3 foll 3rd rows.
1st, 2nd, 3rd, 4th, 5th & 6th sizes only
Using yarn A, work in st st inc every foll 3rd
row to 45(47:53:57:65:69)sts.
7th, 8th & 9th sizes only
Using yarn A, work in st st inc every foll 3rd
row to 49(49:61) sts and then every foll 4th
row to 73(77:83) sts.
All sizes
Cont without further shaping until work
measures
19(20:23:25:28:30.5:35.5:38:40.5)cm from
cast on edge ending with a WS row.
Cast off loosely and evenly.

Cardigan
BACK
Cast on 53(57:63:69:73:79:85:91:99) sts
using 4mm (US 6) needles and yarn A and
work in **moss st** as folls:
Row 1 (RS): K1, (P1,K1) to end.
Row 2: Work as given for row 1.
Rep these 2 rows twice more.
Change to 5mm (US 8) needles and joining
in yarn B and work as given for **sweater**
back from * to **.

Shape shoulders and back neck
Cast off 6(6:7:8:8:9:10:10:12) sts at beg next
2 rows.
Cast off 6(7:7:8:8:9:10:11:12) sts K
11(11:12:12:13:14:14:15:16) turn leaving
rem sts on a holder.
Work each side of neck separately.
Cast off 4 sts, patt to end.
Cast off rem 7(7:8:8:9:10:10:11:12)sts.
With RS rejoin yarn to rem sts cast off centre
7(9:11:13:15:15:17:19:19) sts, K to end.
Complete to match first side rev shaping.

SLEEVES
Cast on 25(25:29:29:33:33:39:39:39) sts
using 4mm (US 6) needles and yarn A.
Work 6 rows in **moss st** as given for back.
Complete as given for sweater sleeve from *.

POCKET LININGS 4 larger sizes only (make 2)
Cast on 19(21:23:23) sts using 5mm (US 8)
needles and yarn A.
Work 30(34:38:38) rows in st st beg with a K
row. Leave sts on a holder.

LEFT FRONT
Cast on 30(32:35:38:40:43:46:49:53) sts
using 4mm (US 6) needles and yarn A.
Girls cardigan
Work 5 rows in **moss st**.
Boys cardigan
Work 2 rows in **moss st**.
Next row (buttonhole row) (RS): Work in
moss st to last 4 sts, K2tog,yon, **moss st** 2.
Next row: Work in **moss st** to end working
into back of loop made on previous row.
Work 1 row.
Girls and boys cardigans
Next row (WS): Moss st 4, leave these sts
on a holder for front band, **moss st** to end.
(26(28:31:34:36:39:42:45:49)sts)
Change to 5mm (US 8) needles.
1st, 2nd, 3rd, 4th & 5th sizes only
Work 38 rows in patt from chart for left front
ending with a WS row.
6th, 7th, 8th & 9th sizes only
Work 30(34:38:38) rows in patt from chart
ending with a WS row.
Place pockets
Next row (RS): Using yarn A, K10(11:12:14)
sts, slip next 19(21:23:23) sts onto a holder
and K across sts from first pocket lining, patt
to end.
6th & 7th sizes only
Cont in patt until chart row 38 completed.
All sizes
Cont in st st using yarn A until work measures
19(21.5:25:27:28.5:33:35.5:40:43.5)cm from
cast on edge.
Shape front neck
Dec 1 st at neck edge on next row and every
foll 3rd row to 19(20:22:24:25:28:30:32:36) sts.
Cont without further shaping until front
matches back to shoulder shaping ending
with a WS row.
Shape shoulders
Cast off 6(6:7:8:8:9:10:10:12)sts at beg next row
and 6(7:7:8:8:9:10:11:12) sts beg foll alt row.

Work 1 row.
Cast off rem 7(7:8:8:9:10:10:11:12) sts.

RIGHT FRONT
Cast on 30(32:35:38:40:43:46:49:53) sts using 4mm (US 6) needles and yarn A.
Boys cardigan
Work 5 rows in **moss st**.
Girls cardigan
Work 2 rows in **moss st**.
Next row (buttonhole row) (RS): Moss st 2, yon, K2tog, **moss st** to end.
Next row: Work in **moss st** to end working into back of loop made on previous row.
Work 1 row.
Girls and boys cardigans
Next row (WS): Moss st to last 4 sts, turn and leave these 4 sts on a holder for front band. (26(28:31:34:36:39:42:45:49)sts)
Change to 5mm (US 8) needles and complete as for left front reversing all shaping and placing of pockets on larger sizes.

MAKING UP
PRESS all pieces as described on the information page.
Sweater
Join right shoulder seam using back stitch.
Neck band
With RS facing, using 4mm (US 6) needles and yarn A, beg at left shoulder, pick up and knit 16(16:16:18:18:18:18:20:20) sts down left front neck, knit across 7(7:9:9:9:9:9:11:11) from holder, pick up and knit 16(16:16:18:18:18:18:20:20) sts up right front neck and 4 sts down side back neck, knit across 11(13:15:17:19:19:21:23:23) sts from holder and pick up and knit 4 sts up side back neck. (58(60:64:70:72:72:74:82:82)sts)
Work 4 rows in **two colour** rib.
Cast off in **rib** using yarn A.
Cardigan
Join both shoulder seams using back stitch.
Buttonband (right front boys, left front girls)

Using 4mm (US 6) needles slip sts from holder onto onto LH needle, join in yarn A and keeping patt correct cont in **moss st** until band fits up front to shoulder and across to centre back when slightly stretched. Slip st into place.
Cast off.
Mark position of 5 buttons the first to match buttonhole in band on oposite front, the last to come 1.5cm from front neck shaping and rem spaced evenly between.
Buttonhole band
Work as for button band with the addition of buttonholes worked as before to correspond with markers.
Pocket tops
Slip sts from holder onto a 4mm (US 6) needle and work 4 rows in **moss st**.
Cast off in **moss st**.
See information page for finishing instructions.

KEY
□ A
☒ B

1st
2nd
3rd
4th
5th
6th
7th
8th
9th

right front — left front
sleeve 1st & 2nd size
sleeve 3rd & 4th sizes
sleeve 5th & 6th size
sleeve 7th 8th & 9th sizes

1st
2nd
3rd
4th
5th
6th
7th
8th
9th

12 rows patt sleeve

Garden Patchwork
by KIM HARGREAVES

YARNS
Rowan Handknit D.K. Cotton

A True Navy	244	2(2:3:3:3:4:4)	50gm
B Ice Water	239	2(2:3:3:3:4:4)	50gm
C Boston Fern	230	1(1:1:1:1:1)	50gm
D Tomato	236	1(1:1:1:1:1)	50gm
E Summer Pud.	243	2(2:2:2:2:2)	50gm
F Gerba	223	1(1:1:1:1:1)	50gm
G Popcorn	229	1(1:1:1:1:1)	50gm
H Surf	225	4(4:5:6:6:7)	50gm
J Raspberry	240	1(1:1:1:1:1)	50gm
L Sea Green	237	1(1:1:1:1:1)	50gm

Sizes
1st(2nd:3rd:4th:5th:6th)
To fit
2-3(3-4:4-6:6-8:8-9:9-10) yrs
Actual width
38(41:44:47:51:55)cm
[15(16:17$\frac{1}{4}$:18$\frac{1}{2}$:20:21$\frac{1}{2}$)ins]

Length
42(45:49.5:53.5:57:61)cm
[16$\frac{1}{2}$(18:19$\frac{1}{2}$:21:22$\frac{1}{2}$:24)ins]
Sleeve length
25(28:30.5:35.5:38:40.5)cm
[10(11:12:14:15:16)ins]

NEEDLES
1 pair 3$\frac{1}{4}$mm (no 10) (US 3) needles
1 pair 4mm (no 8) (US 6) needles

TENSION
20 sts and 28 rows to 10cm measured over patterned stocking stitch using 4mm (US 6) needles

BACK
Cast on 76(82:88:94:102:110) sts using 3$\frac{1}{4}$mm (US 3) needles and yarn E.
Work 6 rows in K2, P2 rib inc 1 st at end of

last row and ending with a WS row.
(77(83:89:95:103:111) sts)
Change to 4mm (US 6) needles, joining in and breaking off colours as required and using the **intarsia** technique described on the information page cont in patt from chart for back until chart row 62 completed ending with a WS row.
Cont in **gingham** patt rep the 12 row patt throughout until work measures 42(45:49.5:53.5:57:61)cm from cast on edge ending with a WS row.
Shape shoulders and back neck
Cast off 7(8:9:10:11:12) sts at beg of next 2 rows.
Cast off 8(9:9:10:11:13), patt 12(13:14:15:16:17) sts, turn leaving rem sts on a holder.
Work each side of neck separately.
Cast off 4 sts, work to end.

Cast off rem 8(9:10:11:12:13) sts.
With RS facing rejoin appropriate yarns to rem sts, cast off centre 23(23:25:25:27:27) sts, patt to end. Complete to match first side.

FRONT
Work as for back until 10(10:10:12:12:12) rows shorter than back to shape shoulder ending with a WS row.
Shape front neck
Patt 32(35:39:43:47:51) sts, turn leaving rem sts on a holder.
Work each side of neck separately.
Cast off 4 sts at beg next row.
Dec 1 st at neck edge on next 3(3:5:6:7:7) rows and 2 foll alt rows.
(23(26:28:31:34:38)sts)
Cont without further shaping until front matches back to shoulder shaping ending with a WS row.
Shape shoulder
Cast off 7(8:9:10:11:12) sts at beg of next

row and 8(9:9:10:11:13) beg foll alt row.
Work 1 row.
Cast off rem 8(9:10:11:12:13) sts.
With RS facing rejoin yarns to rem sts, cast off centre 13(13:11:9:9:9) sts, patt to end.
Complete to match first side.

SLEEVES (both alike)
Cast on 32(36:36:42:42:42) sts using 3¼mm (US 3) needles and yarn E.
Work 5 rows in K2, P2 rib ending with a RS row.
Next row (WS)(inc): Purl, inc 1 st at end of row. (33(37:37:43:43:43)sts)
Change to 4mm (US 6) needles, starting at chart row 43 and working between appropriate markers cont in patt from chart.
Shape sides by inc 1 st at each end of 3rd row, 2(2:2:0:0:0) foll alt rows and then every foll 4th row to 65(73:77:85:89:93) sts, rep the 12 row patt throughout and taking the extra stitches into patt as they occur.

Cont without further shaping until sleeve measures 25(28:30.5:35.5:38:40.5) from cast on edge ending with a WS row.
Cast off loosely and evenly.

MAKING UP
PRESS all pieces as described on the information page.
Join right shoulder seam using back stitch.
Neck band
With RS facing, using 3¼mm (US 3) needles and yarn H, beg at left shoulder, pick up and knit 17(17:17:19:19:19) sts down left front neck, 13(13:11:9:9:9) sts across centre front, 17(17:17:19:19:19) sts up right front neck and 31(31:33:33:35:35) across back neck. (78(78:78:80:82:82)sts)
Work 4 rows in K2, P2 rib.
Cast off evenly in rib.
Join left shoulder seam using back stitch and neck band using edge to edge stitch. See information page for finishing instructions.

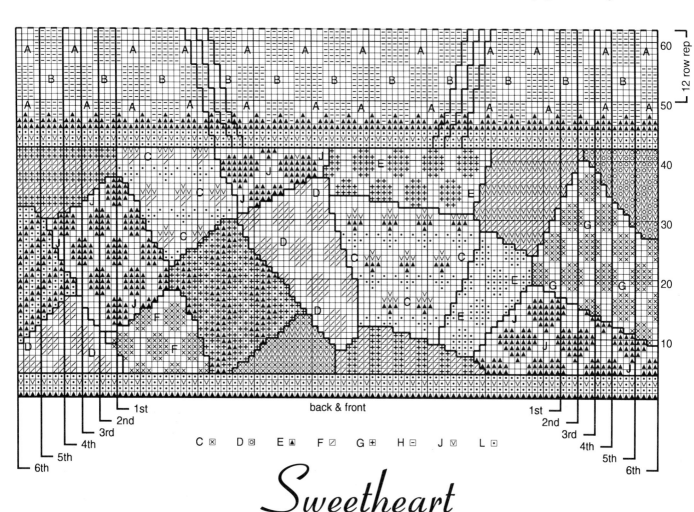

C ⊠   D ◎   E ▲   F ◿   G ⊞   H ⊟   J ☑   L ⊡

Sweetheart

by LOUISA HARDING

YARN
Rowan Handknit D.K cotton

A Soft green	228	6(7:8:8:10:12:14)	50gm
B Gerba	223	1(1:1:1:1:1:2)	50gm
C Raspberry	240	1(1:1:1:1:1:2)	50gm
D Popcorn	229	1(1:1:1:1:1:1)	50gm
E Summer Pud.	243	1(1:1:1:1:1:2)	50gm
F Sea Green	237	1(1:1:1:1:1:1)	50gm

Sizes
1st(2nd:3rd:4th:5th:6th:7th)

To fit
1-2(2-3:3-4:4-6:6-8:8-9:9-10)yrs
Actual width
36(38:41:44:47:51:55)cm
[14(15:16:17¼:18½:20:21½)ins]
Length
38(42:45:49.5:53.5:57:61)cm
[15(16½:17¾:19½:21:22½:24)ins]
Sleeve length
23(25:28:30.5:35.5:38:40.5)cm
[9(10:11:12:14:15:16)ins]

NEEDLES
1 pair 3¼mm (no 10) (US 3) needles
1 pair 4mm (no 8) (US 6) needles

BUTTONS
1st and 2nd sizes only - 5

TENSION
20 sts and 28 rows to 10 cm measured over pattern using
4mm (US 6) needles

Lace Panel 1
Row 1, 3 & 5 (RS): Knit.
Row 2: Knit.
Row 4: P1, (yon, P2tog) to last st, P1.
Row 6: Knit.

Lace Panel 2 (worked over 8 sts)
Row 1 (RS): *K3, yon, K2tog tbl, K3, rep from * to end.
Row 2, 4, 6, 8 & 10: Purl
Row 3: *K2, (yo, K2tog tbl) twice, K2, rep from * to end.
Row 5: *K1, (yo, K2tog tbl) three times, K1, rep from * to end.
Row 7: Work as given for row 3.
Row 9: Work as given for row 1.

BACK
Using 3¼mm (US 3) needles and yarn A, cast on 72(76:82:88:94:102:110) sts and work 4(4:6:6:8:8:8) rows in **garter st** (ie knit every row) Change to 4mm (US 6) needles.
* Work 6 rows of **lace panel 1**.
Work 10 rows of **lace panel 2** setting sts as follows:
Next row (RS): K0(2:1:0:3:3:3) sts, work across row 1 of **lace panel 2** 9(9:10:11:11:12:13) times, K0(2:1:0:3:3:3) sts.
Next row: P0(2:1:0:3:3:3), work across row 2 of **lace panel 2** 9(9:10:11:11:12:13) times, P0(2:1:0:3:3:3) sts.
This sets the sts cont until 10 rows **lace panel 2** completed.
Work 6 rows **lace panel 1**.
Joining in and breaking off yarns as required, using the **intarsia technique** described on the information page and working between markers for appropriate size, work 20 rows in patt from chart.* Rep from * to * until work measures 38(42:45:49.5:53.5:57:61)cm from cast on edge ending with a WS row.
Shape back neck and shoulder
Patt 26(27:29:32:34:37:41), turn, leave rem sts on a holder.
Cast off 3 sts, patt to end.
(23(24:26:29:31:34:38)sts)

Leave sts on a holder.
Rejoin yarn to rem sts, cast off centre 20(22:24:24:26:28:28) sts, patt to end.
Work 1 row.
3rd, 4th, 5th, 6th and 7th sizes only
Complete to match first side.
1st and 2nd sizes only
Cast off 3 sts patt to end.
Using yarn A work 3 rows in st st.
Cast off.

FRONT
Work as given for back until front is 16(16:16:18:18:20:20) rows shorter than back to shoulder ending with a WS row.
Shape front neck
Next row (RS): Patt 30(31:33:36:38:42:46) sts, turn, leave rem sts on a holder.
Dec 1 st at neck edge on next 5(5:5:5:5:6:6) rows and 2 foll alt rows.
(23(24:26:29:31:34:38)sts)
Work without further shaping until front matches back to shoulder shaping ending with a WS row. *
3th, 4th, 5th, 6th and 7th sizes only
Leave sts on a holder.
1st and 2nd sizes only
Work buttonhole band
Purl 2 rows.
Next row (buttonholes)(RS): K3(4), (yon, K2tog, K3) 4 times.
Knit 1 row.
Cast off.
All sizes
Rejoin yarn to rem sts, cast off centre 12(14:16:16:18:18:18) sts, patt to end.
Work as for first side to *.
Leave sts on a holder.

SLEEVES (both alike)
Using 3¼mm (US 3) needles and yarn A, cast on 36(36:40:40:44:44:44) sts work 4(4:6:6:8:8:8) rows in garter st.
Change to 4mm (US 6) needles.
Work in patt as for back until sleeve measures 23(25:28:30.5:35.5:38:40.5)cm from cast on edge, rep the 42 row patt

throughout, setting sts as given below and **AT THE SAME TIME** shape sides by inc 1 st at each end of 2nd row (WS row) and every foll 4th row to 58(64:72:76:82:86:92) sts.
Keeping inc correct throughout set sts as folls:
Work 6 rows of **lace panel 1**.
Work 10 rows of **lace panel 2** as follows:
Next row (RS): K0(0:2:2:4:4:4) sts, work across row 1 of **lace panel 2** 5 times, K0(0:2:2:4:4:4) sts.
Next row: P0(0:2:2:4:4:4), work across row 2 of **lace panel 2** 5 times, P0(0:2:2:4:4:4) sts.
Work 6 rows **lace panel 1**.
Work 20 rows in patt from chart working between markers for appropriate sleeve size.
Rep patt as given above keeping inc correct as set.
Cast off loosely and evenly.

MAKING UP
PRESS all pieces as described on the information page.
Join right shoulder by casting off sts together on the RS.
Neckband
Using 3¼mm (US 3) needles and yarn A, beg at left shoulder, **on first 2 sizes only**, pick up and K3 sts across buttonhole band and 16(16:16:18:18:20:20) sts down right front, 12(14:16:16:18:18:18) sts from centre front, 16(16:16:18:18:20:20) sts up left front and 26(28:30:30:32:34:34) sts from back neck and **on first 2 sizes only** 3 sts from button band. (76(80:78:82:86:92:92)sts)
Knit one row.
1st and 2nd sizes only
Next row (buttonhole row)(RS): K2, yon, K2tog, Knit to end.
All sizes
Knit 2(2:5:5:5:5:5) rows.
Cast off evenly knitwise.
3rd, 4th, 5th, 6th and 7th sizes only
Join left shoulder by casting off sts together on RS.
See information page for finishing instructions.

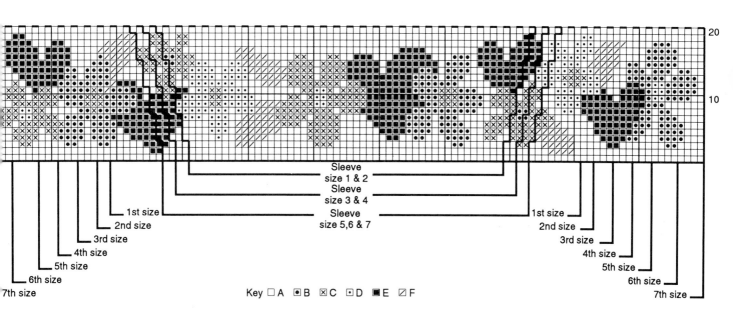

Key □ A ⊡ B ⊠ C ⊡ D ■ E ⊘ F

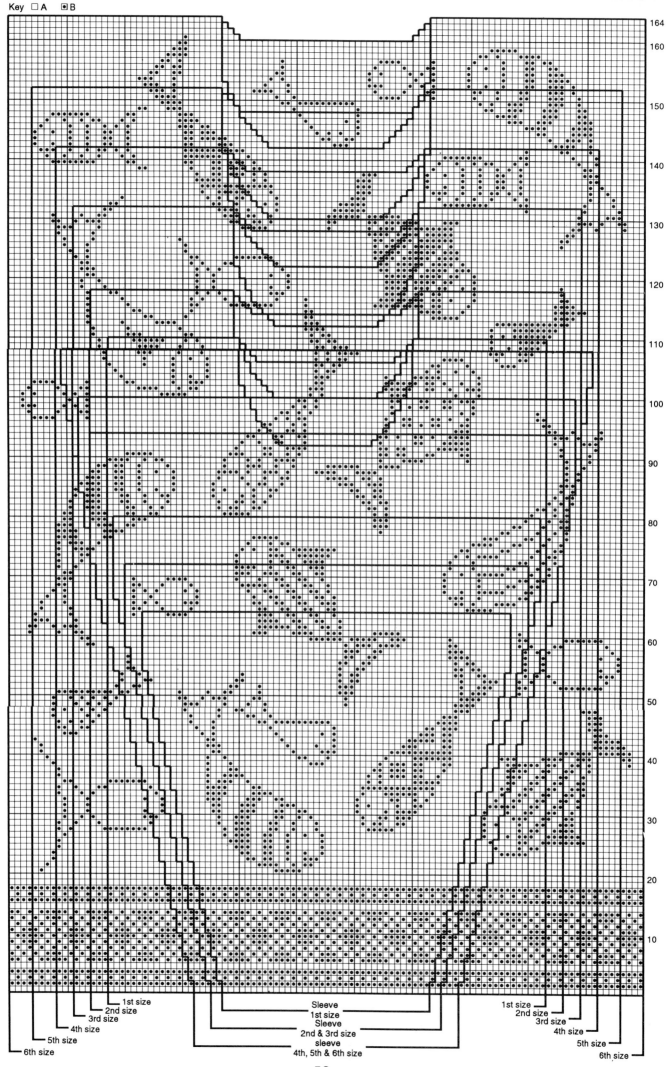

Key ☐ A ☒ B

164
160
150
140
130
120
110
100
90
80
70
60
50
40
30
20
10

1st size
2nd size
3rd size
4th size
5th size
6th size

Sleeve
1st size
Sleeve
2nd & 3rd size
sleeve
4th, 5th & 6th size

1st size
2nd size
3rd size
4th size
5th size
6th size

Fish Sweater

by LOUISA HARDING

YARNS
Rowan Handknit D.K. Cotton

A Ecru	251	6(7:8:9:10:12)	50gm
B Surf	225	3(3:4:4:5:5)	50gm

Sizes
1st(2nd:3rd:4th:5th:6th)
To fit
2-3(3-4:4-6:6-8:8-9:9-10) yrs
Actual width
38(41:44:47:51:55)cm
[15(16:17:18^1/$_2$:20:21^1/$_2$)ins]
Length
42(45:49.5:53.5:57:61)cm
[16^1/$_2$(18:19^1/$_2$:21:22^1/$_2$:24)ins]
Sleeve length
25(28:30.5:35.5:38:40.5)cm
[10(11:12:14:15:16)ins]

NEEDLES
1 pair 3^1/$_4$mm (no 10) (US 3) needles
1 pair 4mm (no 8) (US 6) needles

TENSION
20 sts and 28 rows to 10cm measured over patt stocking stitch using 4mm (US 6) needles

BACK
Cast on 76(82:88:94:102:110) sts using 3^1/$_4$mm (US 3) needles and yarn B.
Row 1 (RS): (K2,P2) to last 0(2:0:2:2:2) sts, K0(2:0:2:2:2).
Row 2: P0(2:0:2:2:2) sts, (K2,P2) to end.
Rep these 2 rows twice more.
Change to 4mm (US 6) needles, joining in yarn A and using a mixture of **fairisle** and **intarsia** techniques as described on the information page cont in patt from chart for back until chart row 106(114:128:138:148:160) completed ending with a WS row.
Shape back neck
Patt 26(28:31:33:36:40) sts, turn leaving rem sts on a holder.
Work each side of neck separately.
Dec 1 st at neck edge on next 3 rows. (23(25:28:30:33:37)sts)
Shape shoulder
Cast off rem sts.
With RS facing slip centre 24(26:26:28:30:30) onto a holder, rejoin yarns to rem sts, work to end. Complete to match first side.

FRONT
Work as for back until chart row 92(100:112:122:130:142) completed ending with a WS row.
Shape front neck
Patt 30(32:35:38:41:45) sts, turn leaving rem sts on a holder.
Work each side of neck separately. Dec 1 st at neck edge on next 4(4:4:5:5:5) rows and 3 foll alt rows. (23(25:28:30:33:37)sts)
Cont without further shaping until front matches back to shape shoulder ending with a WS row.
Shape shoulder
Cast off rem sts.
With RS facing slip centre 16(18:18:18:20:20) sts onto a holder, rejoin appropriate yarns to rem sts, patt to end. Complete as for first side reversing shaping.

SLEEVES (both alike)
Cast on 36(40:40:46:46:46) sts using 3^1/$_4$mm (US 3) needles and yarn B.
Work 6 rows in K2, P2 rib ending with a WS row.
Change to 4mm (US 6) needles and working between appropriate markers, cont in patt from chart until chart row 64(72:80:94:100:108) completed and AT THE SAME TIME shape sides by inc 1 st at each end of 3rd row and every foll 4th row to 64(70:74:80:80:80) sts and then for **3 larger sizes only** every foll 6th row to 82(86:92) sts and ending with a WS row. (64(70:74:82:86:92)sts)
Cast off loosely and evenly.

MAKING UP
PRESS all pieces except ribbing on wrong side using a warm iron over a damp cloth.
Join right shoulder seam using back stitch.
Neck band
With RS facing, using 3^1/$_4$mm (US 3) needles and yarn A, beg at left shoulder, pick up and knit 18(18:20:20:22:22) sts down left front neck, K16(18:18:18:20:20) sts from holder at centre front, pick up and knit 18(18:20:20:22:22) sts up right front neck and 3 sts down back neck, K24(26:26:28:30:30) sts from holder at centre back, pick up and knit 3 sts up back neck to shoulder. (82(86:90:92:100:100)sts)
Work 5 rows in K2, P2 rib. Cast off in rib.
Join left shoulder seam using back stitch and neck band using edge to edge stitch. See information page for finishing instructions.

Mr Pepper

by KIM HARGREAVES

YARNS
Rowan Designer D.K.
4(4:5:6:7:7:9:11:12) 50gm
(Photographed in D.K. 696 and D.K. Tweed Humbug 823)
Sizes
1st(2nd:3rd:4th:5th:6th:7th:8th:9th)
To fit
6mth(9mth:1-2:2-3:3-4:4-6:6-8:8-9:9-10) yrs
Actual width
28(31:34:36.5:41:44:47:51:55)cm
[11(11^1/$_4$:13^1/$_2$:14^1/$_2$:16:17^1/$_2$:18^1/$_2$:20:21^1/$_2$)ins]
Length
29.5(32:37:41:44:48.5:52.5:56:60)cm
[11^1/$_2$(12^1/$_2$:14^1/$_2$:16:17^1/$_4$:19:21:22:23^1/$_2$)ins]
Sleeve length
19(20:23:25:28:30.5:35.5:38:40.5)cm
[7 1/2(8:9:10:11:12:14:15:16)ins]

NEEDLES
1 pair 3^1/$_4$mm (no 10) (US 3) needles
1 pair 4mm (no 8) (US 6) needles

BUTTONS 1st, 2nd, 3rd & 4th sizes only 3 -buttons

TENSION
21 sts and 28 rows to 10cm measured over patterned stocking stitch using 4mm (US 6) needles

BACK
Cast on 59(65:71:77:87:93:99:107:115) using 3^1/$_4$mm (US 3) needles.
Row 1 (RS): K1, (P1, K1) to end.
Row 2: P1, (K1, P1) to end.
Rep these 2 rows once more.
Change to 4mm (US 6) needles and cont in rib pattern setting sts as folls:
Row 1 (RS): K7(0:0:0:3:6:0:0:0), P9(1:4:7:9:9:0:4:8), (K9, P9) 2(3:3:3:4:4:5:5:5) times, K7(9:9:9:3:6:9:9:9), P0(1:4:7:0:0:0:4:8).
Row 2: K0(1:4:7:0:0:0:4:8), P7(9:9:9:3:6:9:9:9), (K9, P9) 2(3:3:3:4:4:5:5:5) times, K9(1:4:7:9:9:0:4:8), P7(0:0:0:3:6:0:0:0).
These 2 rows form the pattern and are repeated throughout.
Cont until work measures 24.5(27:32:36:44:48.5:52.5:56:60)cm from cast on edge ending with a WS row.
1st, 2nd, 3rd & 4th sizes only
Divide for back neck
Patt 28(31:34:37) sts, turn leaving rem sts on a holder.
Work each side of neck separately.
Next row (WS): Cast on 3 sts, K these 3 sts, patt to end.
Next row: Patt to last 3 sts, K3.
Next row: K 3, patt to end.
Rep these last 2 rows until work measures 29.5(32:37:41)cm from cast on edge ending with a RS row.
Shape back neck
Cast off 9(10:11:12) sts at beg of next row and 4 sts beg foll alt row. (18(20:22:24) sts.

– 53 –

Shape shoulder

Leave rem sts on a holder.
Mark position of 2 buttons, the first to come 1.5cm from neck edge the second 2cm down from first.
With RS facing rejoin yarn to rem sts, K3, patt to end.
Next row (WS): Patt to last 3 sts, K3.
Complete as for first side with the addition of 2 button holes worked to correspond with markers as folls.
Buttonhole row (RS): K2tog, yon, K1, patt to end.

5th, 6th, 7th, 8th & 9th sizes only

Shape back neck

Next row (RS): Patt 30(33:35:37:41) sts, turn leaving rem sts on a holder.
Work each side of neck separately.
Cast off 4 sts, patt to end.
(26(29:31:33:37)sts)

Shape shoulder

Leave rem sts on a holder.
With RS facing rejoin yarn to rem sts, cast off centre 27(27:29:33:33) sts, patt to end.
Complete as for first side reversing all shaping.

FRONT

Work as given for back until front is 12(12:12:12:14:14:16:16:16) rows shorter than back to **shape shoulder** ending with a WS row.

Shape front neck

Patt 26(29:31:33:35:38:40:46:50) sts, turn leaving rem sts on a holder.
Work each side of neck separately.
Cast off 4 sts at beg next row and 0(0:0:0:0:0:0:1:1) foll alt row.
Dec 1 st at neck edge on next 3 rows and 1(2:2:2:2:2:2:2:2) foll alt rows.
(18(20:22:24:26:29:31:33:37)sts)
Cont without further shaping until front matches back to **shape shoulder** ending with

a WS row.
Leave sts on a holder.
With RS facing rejoin yarn to rem sts, cast off centre 7(7:9:11:17:17:19:15:15) sts and patt to end.
Complete as for first side reversing shaping.

SLEEVES (both alike)

Cast on 31(31:35:35:39:39:43:43:49) sts using 3¼mm (US 3) needles.
Work 4 rows in K1, P1 rib as given for back.
Change to 4mm (US 6) needles and work in rib pattern setting sts as folls:
Row 1 (RS): K0(0:0:0:0:0:0:0:2), P2(2:4:4:6:6:8:8:9), (K9, P9) 1(1:1:1:1:1:1:1:2) times, K9(9:9:9:9:9:9:9:2), P2(2:4:4:6:6:8:8:0).
Row 2: P0(0:0:0:0:0:0:0:2), K2(2:4:4:6:6:8:8:9), (P9, K9) 1(1:1:1:1:1:1:1:2) times, P9(9:9:9:9:9:9:9:2), K2(2:4:4:6:6:8:8:0).
These 2 rows set the stitches.
Keeping patt correct and taking extra sts into patt as they occur, inc 1 st at each end of next row and every foll 4th row to 51(53:59:65:67:75:71:71:77) sts and then for
5th, 7th, 8th and 9th sizes only every foll 6th row to 71(81:85:93) sts.
(51(53:59:65:71:75:81:85:93)sts)
Cont without further shaping until sleeve measures 19(20:23:25:28:30.5:35.5:38:40.5) cm or length required from cast on edge ending with a WS row.
Cast off in pattern.

MAKING UP

PRESS all pieces as described on the information page.

1st, 2nd, 3rd & 4th sizes only

Join both shoulder seams by casting off stitches together on RS.

Neck band

With RS facing, using 3¼mm (US 3) needles,

beg at left back neck opening, pick up and knit 13(14:15:16) sts across back neck to shoulder, 15 sts down left front neck, 7(7:9:11) sts across centre front, 15 sts up right front neck, and 13(14:15:16) across right back neck. (63(65:69:73)sts)
Next row (WS): K3, P1, (K1, P1) to last 3 sts, K3.
Next row: K3, K1, (P1, K1) to last 3 sts, K3.
Keeping rib patt correct work 4 rows more and AT THE SAME TIME make a buttonhole on 4th row to correspond with others.
Cast off in rib.

5th, 6th, 7th, 8th & 9th sizes only

Join right shoulder seam by casting off stitches together on RS.

Turtle neck

Please note the stitches are picked up so that the rib patt follows through into collar.
With RS facing, starting at left shoulder seam and using 4mm (US 6) needles, pick up and knit 10(12:14:15:15) sts over first panel of rev st st, 9 sts over st st, 9 sts over rev st st, 9 sts over st st, 10(12:14:15:15) sts to shoulder, 3(4:6:7:7) sts over rev st st, 9 sts over st st, 9 sts over rev st st, 9 sts over st st and 3(4:6:7:7) sts to end. (80(86:94:98:98)sts)
Keeping rib patt correct cont until collar measures 12cm.
Cast off in patt.

Crew neck

With RS facing, using 3¼mm (US 3) needles, pick up and knit 14(17:19:21:21) sts down left front neck, 17(17:19:15:15) sts across centre front 14(17:19:21:21) sts up right front neck and 35(35:37:41:41) sts across back neck. (80(86:94:98:98)sts)
Work 2.5cm in K1, P1 rib.
Cast off in rib.
Join left shoulder seam by casting off stitches together on RS.
See information page for finishing instructions.

Jammy Dodger

by LOUISA HARDING

YARN

Rowan Designer D.K
4(4:5:6:9:9:10:10) 50gm
(Photographed in 686)

Sizes

1st(2nd:3rd:4th:5th:6th:7th:8th:9th)

To fit

6mth(9th:1-2:2-3:3-4:4-6:6-7:8-9:9-10) yrs

Actual width

30(32:35:38:41:44:47.5:51:55)cm
[11½(12½:13¾:15:16:17¼:18½:20:21½) ins]

Length

30.5(33:38:42:45:49.5:53.5:57:61)cm
[12(13:15:16½:18:19½:21:22½:24)ins]

Sleeve length

19(20:23:25:28:30.5:35.5:38:40.5)cm
[7½(8:9:10:11:12:14:15:16)ins]

NEEDLES

1 pair 3¼mm (no 10) (US 3) needles
1 pair 4mm (no 8) (US 6) needles

BUTTONS 3(3:3:3:3:4:4:4:4)

TENSION

22 sts and 30 rows to 10cm measured over pattern using 4mm (US 6) needles

BACK

Cast on 65(71:77:83:89:97:105:113:121) using 3¼mm (US 3) needles and work in **broken rib** as folls:
Row 1 (RS): Knit
Row 2: K1(0:1:0:1:1:1:1:1), (P1, K1) to last 0(1:0:1:0:0:0:0:0) sts, P1.
Rep these 2 rows 4 times more.
Change to 4mm (US 6) needles and beg and ending where indicated work in patt from chart working the 8 sts patt 8(8:9:10:11:12:13:14:15) times across row and rep the 10 row patt throughout cont until work measures 30.5(33:38:42:45:49.5:53.5:57:61)cm from cast

on edge ending with a WS row.

Shape back neck

Patt 24(26:28:30:32:35:38:41:45) sts, turn, leave rem sts on a holder.
Next row: Cast off 3 sts, patt to end.
(21(23:25:27:29:32:35:38:42)sts)
Cast off evenly.
Rejoin yarn to rem sts. Cast off centre 17(19:21:23:25:27:29:31:31) sts, patt to end.
Complete to match first side.

FRONT

Work as for back until work measures 20(20.5:24.5:27.5:29.5:32.5:35.5:38:41)cm from cast on edge, ending with a WS row.

Divide for front neck

Next row (RS): Patt 30(33:36:39:42:46:50:54:58) sts, turn, leave rem sts on a holder.

Keeping patt correct cont until work measures
25(27.5:32.5:36.5:39.5:43.5:47.5:51:55)
from cast on edge ending with a RS row.
Next row: Cast off 4(4:4:4:4:4:6:6:6) sts, patt to end.
Dec 1 st at neck edge on next
3(4:5:6:7:7:6:7:7) rows and
2(2:2:2:2:3:3:3:3) foll alt rows.
(21(23:25:27:29:32:35:38:42)sts)
Work without further shaping until front matches back to shoulder shaping ending with a WS row.
Cast off evenly.
With RS facing return to rem sts, slip centre 5 sts onto a holder, rejoin yarn and patt to end.
Complete to match first side rev all shaping.

SLEEVES (both alike)
Using 3¼mm (US 3) needles cast on
31(31:33:33:39:39:47:47:47) sts work 10 rows in **broken rib** as folls:
Row 1 (RS): Knit.
Row 2: K1(1:1:0:0:0:1:1:1), (P1, K1) to last 0(0:0:1:1:1:0:0:0) sts, P0(0:0:1:1:1:0:0:0).
Change to 4mm (US 6) needles and cont in patt from chart working between markers for appropriate size and rep the 10 row patt throughout and AT THE SAME TIME shape sides by inc 1 st at each end of 3rd row and every foll 3rd row to
57(59:65:71:71:71:55:55:55) sts and then for **5 larger sizes only** every foll 4th row to
79(83:91:95:101)sts.
57(59:65:71:79:83:91:95:101)sts)
Cont without further shaping until work measures 19(20:23:25:28:30.5:35.5:38:40.5)cm from cast on edge ending with a WS row.
Cast off evenly

MAKING UP
PRESS all pieces as described on the information page.
Join both shoulder seams using back st.
Button band
Place a marker through 5 sts at centre front.
With RS facing, using 3¼mm (US 3) needles rejoin yarn to 5 sts at centre front, leaving marker in place.
Work in **broken rib** as for back, until band fits, when slightly stretched, to beg neck shaping ending with a WS row, cast off.
Slip st into place on left side for girls, right side for boys.
Mark position of 3(3:3:3:3:4:4:4:4) buttons, first to come 1.5cm from marker, the last to come 1cm down from neck shaping, the others spaced evenly between.
Buttonhole band
With RS facing rejoin yarn to same sts and work as given for button band working buttonholes to correspond with button markers as follows.
Buttonhole row (RS): Patt 2, yon, patt 2 tog, patt 1.
Slip stitch into place on opposite side.
Polo Collar
Using 3 1/4mm (no 10) needles cast on 67(69:71:73:77:81:87:95:95).
Row 1 (RS): Knit.
Row 2: K1, (P1, K1) to end.
Rep these 2 rows 4 times more.
Next row (RS): K2, K into the front, back and front of next st, knit to last 3 sts, K into front, back and front of next st, K2.
Work 5 rows in patt.
Rep last 6 rows until work measures 6(6.5:7:7.5:8:8.5:9:9.5:10)cm ending with a WS row.

Cast off evenly in rib.
Slip st cast on edge of collar into place, starting end ending half way across bands and matching centre of collar to centre back neck.
See information page for finishing instructions.

Key
☐ K on RS, P on WS
⊡ P on RS, K on WS

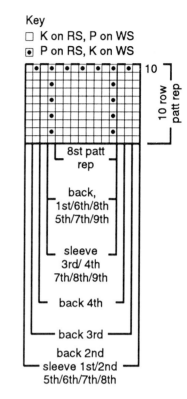

10
10 row patt rep

8st patt rep

back,
1st/6th/8th
5th/7th/9th

sleeve
3rd/ 4th
7th/8th/9th

back 4th

back 3rd

back 2nd
sleeve 1st/2nd
5th/6th/7th/8th

Riddler

by LOUISA HARDING

YARN
Rowan Recyled Chunky or Chunky Tweed

Jacket knitted in two colours
A. Tin   895   1(2:2:2:2:3:3) 100gm
B. Steel   898   4(5:6:6:7:8) 100gm

Jacket knitted in one colour
4(5:5:5:7:8) 100gm
(Photographed in Polar 879)

Sizes
1st(2nd:3rd:4th:5th:6th)
To fit
2-3(3-4:4-5:6-8:8-9:9-10) yrs
Actual width
38(41:44:46.5:51:55)cm
[15(16:17¼:18¼:20:21½)ins]
Length
38(41:44:47:51:55)cm
[15(16:17¼:18½:20:21½)ins]
Sleeve length
28(31:33.5:38:41:44)cm
[11(12¼:13¼:15:16:17¼)ins]

NEEDLES
1 pair 5mm (no 6) (US 8) needles
1 pair 5½mm (no 5) (US 9) needles
1 pair 6mm (no 4) (US 10) needles

BUTTONS 7 - buttons

TENSION
14 sts and 20 rows measured over stocking stitch using 6mm (US 10) needles

BACK
For one colour garment ignore colour changes.
Cast on 49(53:55:59:63:69) sts using 5mm (US 8) needles and yarn A, work in **moss st** as folls:
Row 1 (RS): (K1, P1), to last st, K1.
Rep this row 5 times more.
Change to 6mm (US 10) needles and yarn B.
Work 8(8:8:8:10:14) rows in st st beg with a K row. Inc 1 st at each end of next row and 1(1:2:2:3:3) foll 16th(16th:12th:12th:10th:10th) rows. (53(57:61:65:71:77)sts)
Cont without further shaping until work

measures 22(23:25:27:30:32) cm from cast on edge ending with a WS row.
Shape armhole
Cast off 4(4:4:4:5:5) sts at the beg next 2 rows. (45(49:53:57:61:67)sts)
Work 2(2:2:2:4:4) rows.
Change to yarn A.
Next row (RS): Knit.
Change to 5 1/2mm (US 9) needles cont in **moss st** until work measures 38(41:44:47:51:55)cm from cast on edge ending with a WS row.
Shape back neck
Patt 15(17:18:20:21:24) sts, turn leaving rem sts on a holder.
Work each side of neck separately.
Cast off 2 sts, patt to end.
Cast off rem 13(15:16:18:19:22) sts.
With RS facing rejoin yarn to rem sts, cast off centre 15(15:17:17:19:19) sts, patt to end.
Complete to match the first side.

POCKET LININGS (work 2)
Cast on 13(13:15:15:17:17) sts using 6mm (US 10) needles using yarn B.

Work 14(14:16:18:18:20) rows in st st beg with a K row.
Leave sts on a holder.

LEFT FRONT
Cast on 36(38:39:41:43:46) sts using 5mm (US 8) needles and yarn A.
Work 2 rows in **moss st**.
Boys jacket
Next row (buttonhole row)(RS): Patt 2, yon, patt 2tog, patt to last 4 sts, patt 2tog, yon, patt 2.
Girls jacket
Next row (buttonhole row)(RS): Patt 2, yon, patt 2tog, patt to end.
Boys and girls
Work 2 rows more in **moss st**.
Row 6 (WS): Patt 5 leave these sts on a holder for front band, patt to last 6 sts, cast off 6, break yarn. (25(27:28:30:32:35)sts)
Change to 6mm (US 10) needles and yarn B and work 8(8:8:8:10:14) rows in st st beg with a K row.
Inc 1 st at side edge of next row and 1(1:2:2:3:3) foll 16th(16th:12th:12th:10th:10th) rows as for back and AT THE SAME TIME when 14(14:16:18:18:20) rows of st st have been completed place pockets as folls:
Place pocket
Row 15(15:17:19:19:21)(RS): K6(7:6:7:8:9) sts, slip next 13(13:15:15:17:17) sts onto a holder, K across sts for pocket lining, K to end. Complete shaping. (27(29:31:33:36:39)sts)
Cont without further shaping until front matches back to armhole shaping ending with a WS row.
Shape armhole
Cast off 4(4:4:4:5:5) sts at beg next row. (23(25:27:29:31:34)sts)
Work 3(3:3:3:5:5) rows.
Change to yarn A.
Next row: Knit.
Change to 5¹/₂mm (US 9) needles and cont in

moss st until front is 13(13:15:15:15:15) rows shorter than back to shoulder ending with a RS row.
Shape front neck
Cast off 4(4:4:4:5:5) sts beg next row, patt to end.
Dec 1 st at neck edge on next 3(3:4:4:4:4) rows and 3 foll alt rows. (13(15:16:18:19:22)sts)
Cont without further shaping until front matches back to shoulder ending with a WS row. Cast off.

RIGHT FRONT
Cast on 36(38:39:41:43:46) sts using 5mm (US 8) needles and yarn A.
Work 2 rows in **moss st**.
Girls jacket
Next row (buttonhole row)(RS): Patt 2, yon, patt 2tog, patt to last 4 sts, patt 2tog, yon, patt 2.
Boys jacket
Next row (buttonhole row)(RS): Patt to the last 4 sts, yon, patt 2tog, yon, patt 2.
Boys and girls
Work 2 rows more in **moss st**.
Row 6 (WS): Cast off 6 sts, patt to last 5 sts, turn leaving rem sts on a holder for front band break yarn. (25(27:28:30:32:35)sts)
Change to 6mm (US 10) needles and yarn B and complete as for left front reversing placing of pocket and all shaping.

SLEEVES (both alike)
Cast on 27(27:29:29:31:31) sts using 5mm (US 8) needles and yarn A, work 6 rows in **moss st** as given for back.
Change to 6mm (US 10) needles and yarn B and cont in st st beg with a K row, inc 1 st each end of 3rd row and every foll 5(4:4:4:5:4) row to 43(51:53:55:57:63)sts.
Cont without further shaping until work measures 28(31:33.5:38:41:44)cm from cast on edge ending with a WS row.
Cast off loosely and evenly.

MAKING UP
PRESS all pieces as described on the information page.
Join both shoulder seams using back stitch.
Button band (right front for boys, left front for girls)
Using 5mm (US 8) needles slip 5 sts from holder onto LH needle, rejoin yarn A and keeping patt correct cont in **moss st** until bands fits up front to start of neck shaping when slightly stretched. Slip st into place. Cast off.
Mark the position of 5 buttons, the first to come opposite the buttonhole on opposite band, the last to come 1.5cm below start of neck shaping the other 3 spaced evenly between.
Buttonhole band
Work as for button band with the addition of buttonholes worked as before to correspond with markers.
Pocket tops (both alike)
With RS facing and using 5mm (US 8) needles slip sts from holder onto LH needle. Using yarn B work 3 rows in **moss st**.
Cast off evenly in patt.
Collar
Using yarn B cast on 45(45:49:49:51:51) sts using 5mm (US 8) needles and work 4(4:6:6:8:8) rows in **moss st**.
Next row inc (RS): Patt 3, K into front, back & front of next st (2 sts made), Patt to last 4 sts, inc as before, patt 3.
Work 3 rows in patt.
Rep these 4 rows until collar measures 7(7:8:8:9:9) cm from beg ending with a WS row.
Cast off evenly in patt.
See information page for finishing instructions overlapping buttonhole extension on lower front side edges onto back, sewing buttons into place on back to correspond with buttonholes.

Patchwork Blanket

by KIM HARGREAVES

YARN
Rowan Designer D.K.

A	649	2 x	50gm
B	664	1 x	50gm
C	689	1 x	50gm
D	652	1 x	50gm
E	65	1 x	50gm
F	693	1 x	50gm
G	665	2 x	50gm
H	694	1 x	50gm
J	685	1 x	50gm

NEEDLES
1 pair 3¹/₄mm (no 10) (US3) needles
1 pair 4mm (no 8) (US 6) needles

TENSION
22 sts and 30 rows to 10cm measured over patterned stocking stitch using 4mm (US 6) needles

Blanket
Cast on 133 sts using 3 1/4mm (US 6) needles and yarn A.
Work 5 rows in **moss st** as folls:
Row 1 (RS): K1, (P1, K1) to end.
Rep this row 4 times more.
Next row (WS): Patt 5, leave these 5 sts on a holder, **purl** to last 5 sts, turn leaving rem 5 sts on a holder. (123sts)
Change to 4mm (US 6) needles and joining in a breaking off colours as required work 212 rows in patt from chart, using the **intarsia** technique described on the information page.
Left side edging
With RS facing and using 3¹/₄mm (US 3) needles, slip sts from holder at left side onto left hand needle. Join in yarn A, and keeping **moss st** patt correct patt across row inc 1 st at **inside** edge. (6sts)

Cont in **moss st** until band fits to top of work when slightly stretched ending with a WS row.
Break yarn but leave sts on a holder.
Slip stitch into place.
Right side edging
Work as given for left side edging ending with a WS row, leave sts on needle, **do not break yarn**.
Top edging
With RS facing using 3¹/₄mm (US 3) needles and yarn A. Work across 6 sts of right side edge as folls: **moss st** 4, patt 2tog, then knit across 123 sts of centre panel and work across 6 sts of left side edge as folls: patt 2tog, **moss st**, 4. (133sts)
Work 5 rows in **moss st**.
Cast off in patt.

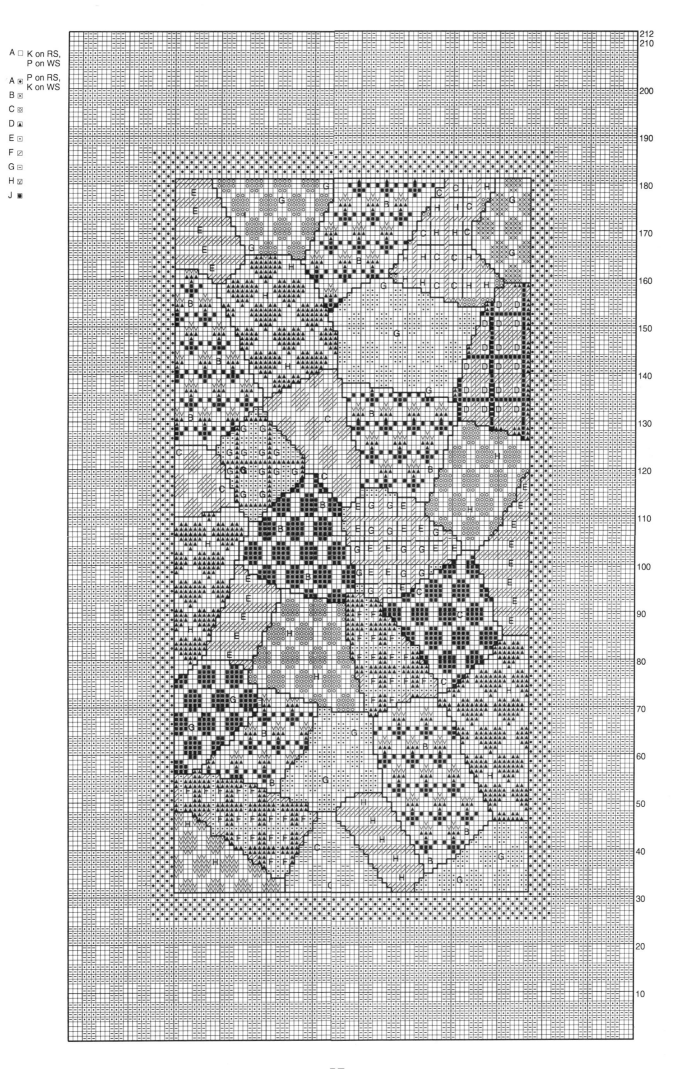

Primrose Cardigan

by LOUISA HARDING

YARNS

Rowan Handknit D.K. Cotton

A Gerba	223	2(2:2:3:3:3:3)	50gm
B Lime	234	1(2:2:2:2:3:3)	50gm
C Boston Fern	230	2(2:2:2:2:3:3)	50gm
D Soft Green	228	1(1:2:2:2:2:2)	50gm
E Summer Pud.	243	1(1:2:2:3:3:3)	50gm
F Raspberry	240	1(1:2:2:2:3:3)	50gm

Sizes

1st(2nd:3rd:4th:5th:6th:7th)

To fit

1-2(2-3:3-4:4-6:6-8:8-9:9-10) yrs

Actual width

33(35:37.5:40.5:44:47.5:51.5)cm
[13(13^1/$_2$:14^1/$_2$:16:17:18^1/$_2$:20)ins]

Length

29(31:33:35.5:38:41.5:43)cm
[11^1/$_2$(12^1/$_4$:13:14:15:16^1/$_4$:17)ins]

Sleeve length

24(27:30:32.5:37.5:40:42.5)cm
[9^1/$_2$(10^1/$_2$:12:12^3/$_4$:14^3/$_4$:15^3/$_4$:16^3/$_4$)ins]

NEEDLES

1 pair 3^1/$_4$mm (no 10) (US 3) needles
1 pair 4mm (no 8) (US 6) needles

BUTTONS 4(5:5:5:6:6:6)

TENSION

22 sts and 25 rows to 10cm measured over patterned stocking stitch using 4mm (US 6) needles

BACK

Cast on 72(76:82:88:96:104:112) sts using 3^1/$_4$mm (US 3) needles and yarn C.
Work 8 rows in K2, P2 rib ending with a WS and inc 1 st at end of last row.
(73(77:83:89:97:105:113)sts)
Change to 4mm (US 6) needles, joining in and breaking off colours as required and using the **fairisle** technique described on the information page cont in pattn from chart for back, rep the 48 pattn row throughout until work measures 29(31:33:35.5:38:41.5:43) cm from cast on edge ending with a WS row.

Shape shoulders and back neck

Patt 26(27:29:32:34:37:41) sts, turn leaving rem sts on a holder.
Work each side of neck separately.
Cast off 3 sts, patt to end.
Cast off rem 23(24:26:29:31:34:38) sts.
Work each side of neck separately.
With RS facing rejoin appropriate yarns to rem sts, cast off centre 21(23:25:25:29:31:31) sts, patt to end.
Complete to match first side.

POCKET LINING (make 2)

Cast on 18(18:20:20:22:22:22) sts using 4mm (US 6) needles and yarn A work 16(16:16:18:18:20:20) rows in st st ending with a WS row. Leave sts on a holder.

LEFT FRONT

Cast on 36(38:42:44:48:52:56) sts using

3^1/$_4$mm (US 3) needles and yarn C.
Work 8 rows in K2, P2 rib ending with a WS row and inc 1 st at end of last row on 1st, 2nd, 4th, 5th, 6th and 7th sizes.
37(39:42:45:49:53:57)sts)
Change to 4mm (US 6) needles and work in pattn from chart until 16(16:16:18:18:20:20) chart rows completed ending with a WS row.

Place pockets

Patt 9(10:11:12:13:15:17) sts, slip next 18(18:20:20:22:22:22) sts onto a holder, patt across first pocket lining, patt to end.
Cont in pattn until work measures 12(13:14.5:15.5:16:17.5:18.5)cm from cast on edge ending with a WS row.

Shape front neck

Dec 1 st at neck edge on next row and 5(4:6:5:5:4:5) foll alt rows, then every foll 3rd row to 23(24:26:29:31:34:38) sts.
Cont without further shaping until front matches back to shoulder ending with a WS row.
Cast off.

RIGHT FRONT

Work as for left front following pattn for right front, reversing placing of pocket and all shaping.

SLEEVES (both alike)

Cast on 36(36:40:40:46:46:46) sts using 3^1/$_4$mm (US 3) needles and yarn C.
Work 8 rows in K2, P2 rib inc 1 st at end of

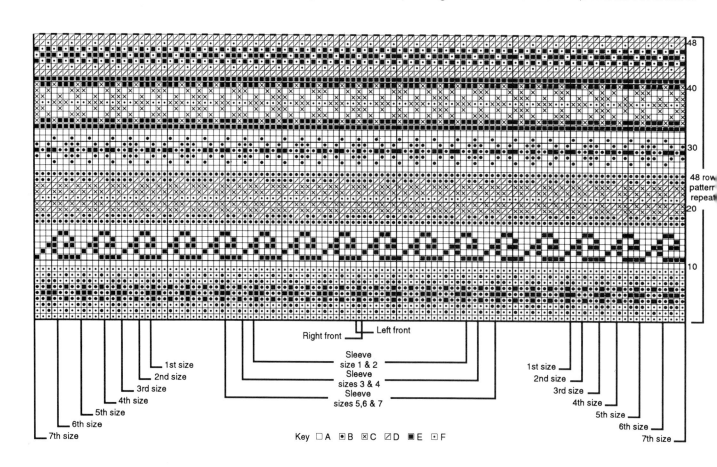

Right front — Left front

Sleeve size 1 & 2
Sleeve sizes 3 & 4
Sleeve sizes 5,6 & 7

1st size
2nd size
3rd size
4th size
5th size
6th size
7th size

1st size
2nd size
3rd size
4th size
5th size
6th size
7th size

48 row pattern repeat

Key □A ■B ⊠C ☑D ▪E ⊡F

last row. (37(37:41:41:47:47:47)sts)
Change to 4mm (US 6) needles and working between appropriate markers, cont in patt from chart and taking sts into patt as they occur shape sides by inc 1 st at each end of 3rd row and every foll 3rd row to 65(71:79:85:77:77:77) sts and then for 3 larger sizes every foll 4th row to 91(95:101) sts.
(65(71:79:85:91:95:101)sts)
Work without further shaping until sleeve measures 24(27:30:32.5:37.5:40:42.5)cm from cast on edge ending with a WS row.
Cast off loosely and evenly.

MAKING UP
PRESS all pieces as described on the information page.
Join shoulder seams using back stitch.
Button band
With RS of left front facing, using 3¼mm (US 3) needles and yarn C pick up and K26(28:30:32:34:38:40) sts from cast on edge to beg neck shaping, 40(42:44:48:52:56:58) sts to shoulder and 10(10:12:12:14:14:14) sts across to centre back neck. (76(80:86:92:100:108:112)sts)
Work 4 rows in K2, P2 rib.
Cast off in rib.

Buttonhole band
Work to match button band with the addition of 4(5:5:5:6:6:6) button holes worked on 2nd row as folls:
Row 2 (buttonholes)(RS): Rib 2, (yon, K2tog, rib 5(4:4:5:4:4:5) sts) 3(4:4:4:5:5:5) times, yon, K2tog, rib to end.
Pocket tops (both alike)
With RS facing slip stitches from holder onto a 3¼mm (US 3) needle and using yarn B knit one row.
Work 2 rows in K2, P2 rib. Cast off in rib.
See information page for finishing instructions.

Cuddle
by LOUISA HARDING

YARN
Rowan Designer D.K.
Sweater or cardigan
4(5:6:6:8:9:10:10:11) 50gm
(Sweater photographed in Cream 649 cardigan in 652)

Sizes - Sweater and cardigan
1st(2nd:3rd:4th:5th:6th:7th:8th:9th)
To fit
6mth(9mth:1-2:2-3:3-4:4-6:6-8:8-9:9-10) yrs
Actual width
29(32:35:38:41:44:47:51:55)cm
[11½(12½:14:15:16:17:18½:20:21½)ins]
Length
30.5(33:38:42:45:48:51:53.5:56)cm
[12(13:15:16½:18:19½:21:22½:24)ins]
Sleeve length
19(20:23:25:28:30.5:35.5:38:40.5)cm
[7½(8:9:10:11:12:14:15:16)ins]

NEEDLES
1 pair 3¼mm (no 10)(US 3) needles
1 pair 4mm (no 8) (US 6) needles

BUTTONS (cardigan only) - 5(5:5:5:6:6:7:7:7:7)

TENSION
26 sts and 30 rows to 10cm measured over cable pattern using 4mm (US 6) needles

Panel 1 (10 stitches)
Row 1 (RS): P2, K6, P2.
Row 2 and all WS rows: K2, P6, K2.
Row 3: P2, C6B, P2.
Rows 5 and 7: As row 1.
Row 9: P2, C6F, P2.
Row 11: Work as row 1.
Row 12: Work as row 2.
These 12 rows form the pattern and are repeated throughout.

Panel 2 (11 stitches)
Row 1 (RS): P1, K2, P2, K4, P2.
Row 2: K2, P4, K2, P2, K1.
Row 3: P1, T3F, T3B, T3F, P1.
Row 4: K1, P2, K2, P4, K2.
Row 5: P2, C4B, P2, K2, P1.
Row 6: Work as row 4.
Row 7: P1, T3B, T3F, T3B, P1.
Row 8: Work as row 2.
Row 9: P1, K2, P2, C4F, P2.

Row 10: Work as row 2.
Rows 3 to 10 form the pattern and are repeated throughout.

Panel 3 (12 stitches)
Row 1 (RS): P2, K8, P2.
Row 2: K2, P8, K2.
Row 3: P2, C4B, C4F, P2.
Rows 4 and 6: Work as row 2.
Row 5: Work as row 1.
Row 7: Work as row 3.
Row 8: K2, P2, K4, P2, K2.
Row 9: P1, T3B, P4, T3F, P1.
Rows 10, 12 and 14: K1, P2, K6, P2, K1.
Rows 11 and 13: P1, K2, P6, K2, P1.
Row 15: P1, T3F, P4, T3B, P1.
Row 16: Work as row 8.
Row 17: P2, C4F, C4B, P2.
Row 18: Work as row 2.
Row 19: Work as row 3.
Row 20: Work as row 2.
These 20 rows form the pattern and are repeated throughout.

Panel 4 (15 stitches)
Rows 1 and 3 (RS): P1, K3, P1, (K1, P1) 3 times, K3, P1.
Rows 2 and 4: K1, P3, P1, (K1, P1) 3 times, P3, K1.
Row 5: P1, C6F, K1, C6B, P1.
Rows 6, 8, 10 and 12: K1, P13, K1.
Rows 7, 9 and 11: P1, K13, P1.
Row 13: P1. C6B, K1, C6F, P1.
Row 14: Work as row 2.
Row 15: Work as row 1.
Row 16: Work as row 2.
These 16 rows form the pattern and are repeated throughout.

Pattern note: To work the cable panels, foll either the instructions given above or work from the chart. Work between markers at bottom of chart for size required, placing the panels as indicated, repeating the different pattern repeats throughout and working any stitches at side edge, which do not form a complete pattern, in reverse stocking stitch.

Sweater
BACK
Cast on 68(74:80:86:92:98:104:114:122) using 3¼mm (US 3) needles.

Work 4(4:5:5:5:5:5:7:7)cm in K2, P2, rib ending with a RS row.
*Next row (WS)(inc): Rib 4(5:5:7:4:1:7:3:1), (M1, rib 10(8:7:6:6:6:5:6:6), 6(8:10:12:14:16:18:18:20) times, M1, rib 4(5:5:7:4:1:7:3:1).
(75(83:91:99:107:115:123:133:143)sts)
Change to 4mm (US 6) needles and working between markers for appropriate size cont in cable pattern setting the stitches for the panels as indicated, see **pattern note**.
Cont rep the panel rows throughout until work measures 30.5(33:38:42:45:48:51:53.5:56)cm from cast on edge ending with a WS row.
Shape shoulders and back neck
Cast off 7(8:9:10:11:12:13:14:16) sts at beg next 2 rows.
Cast off 8(9:10:11:11:13:13:15:16) sts, patt 11(12:13:14:15:16:17:18:20) sts, turn leaving rem sts on a holder.
Work each side of neck separately.
Cast off 3 sts patt to end.
Cast off rem 8(9:10:11:12:13:14:15:17) sts.
With RS facing slip centre 23(25:27:29:33:33:37:39:39) sts onto a holder, rejoin yarn and pattern to end.
Complete to match first side rev all shaping.

FRONT
Work as for back until work measures 25(27.5:32.5:36.5:39.5:42:45:47.5:50)cm from cast on edge ending with a WS row.
Shape front neck
Pattern 31(34:38:42:45:49:52:56:61) sts, turn leaving rem sts on a holder.
Work each side of neck separately.
Dec 1 st at neck edge on next 6(6:7:8:9:9:9:9:9) rows and 2(2:2:2:2:2:3:3:3) foll alt rows. (23(26:29:32:34:38:40:44:49)sts)
Cont without further shaping until front matches back to shoulder shaping ending with a WS row.
Shape shoulder
Cast off 7(8:9:10:11:12:13:14:16) sts at beg next row and 8(9:10:11:11:13:13:15:16) sts beg foll alt row. Work 1 row.
Cast off rem 8(9:10:11:12:13:14:15:17) sts.
Return to rem sts and with RS facing slip centre 13(15:15:15:17:17:19:21:21) sts onto a holder, pattern to end.
Complete as for first side reversing shaping.

SLEEVES (both alike)
Cast on 32(32:34:34:38:38:44:44:44) sts using 3¹/₄mm (US 3) needles and work 8(8:10:10:10:10:10:14:14) cm in K2, P2 rib ending with a RS row.
Next row (WS)(inc): Rib 4(4:2:2:3:3:2:2:2), (M1, rib 6(6:5:5:4:4:4:4:4), 4(4:6:6:8:8:10:10:10) times, M1, rib 4(4:2:2:3:3:2:2:2).
(37(37:41:41:47:47:55:55:55)sts)
Change to 4mm (US 6) needles and working between markers for appropriate size cont in cable pattern setting the stitches for the panels as indicated, see **pattern note** and AT THE SAME TIME shape sides by inc 1 st at each end of 3rd row and every foll 4th(3rd:3rd:3rd:3rd:3rd:3rd:3rd:3rd) row to 57(61:69:75:85:91:67:81:93) sts and then for **7th, 8th and 9th sizes only** every foll 4th row to 97(103:111) sts, taking extra sts into reverse st st as they occur.
(57(61:69:75:85:91:97:103:111)sts)
Cont without further shaping until work measures 23(24:28:30:33:35.5:40.5:45:47.5)cm from cast on edge. (This allows for turn back cuff).
Cast off in pattern.

Cardigan
BACK
Cast on 68(74:80:86:92:98:104:114:122) using 3¹/₄mm (US 3) needles.
Work 2.5cm in K2, P2 rib ending with a RS row.
Complete as given for sweater back from * but casting off stitches at centre back neck.

SLEEVES (both alike)
Work as given for sweater sleeves.

LEFT FRONT
Cast on 34(37:40:43:46:49:52:57:61) using 3¹/₄mm (US 3) needles.
Work 2.5cm in K2, P2 rib ending with a RS row.
Next row (WS)(inc): Rib 2(3:3:4:2:5:4:2:6), (M1, rib 10(8:7:6:6:5:5:6:5), 3(4:5:6:7:8:9:9:10) times, M1, rib 2(2:2:3:2:4:3:1:5).

(38(42:46:50:54:58:62:67:72)sts)
Change to 4mm (US 6) needles and working between markers for appropriate size cont in cable pattern setting the stitches for panels as indicated.
Cont rep the panel rows throughout until work measures 25(27.5:32.5:36.5:39.5:42:45:47.5:50)cm from cast on edge ending with a RS row.
Shape front neck
Next row (WS): Cast off 7(8:8:8:9:9:10:11:11) sts at beg next row patt to end.
Dec 1 st at neck edge on next 6(6:7:8:9:9:9:9:9) rows and 2(2:2:2:2:2:3:3:3) foll alt rows.
(23(26:29:32:34:38:40:44:49)sts)
Cont without further shaping until front matches back to shoulder shaping ending with a WS row.
Shape shoulder
Cast off 7(8:9:10:11:12:13:14:16) sts at beg next row and 8(9:10:11:11:13:13:15:16) sts beg foll alt row.
Work 1 row.
Cast off rem 8(9:10:11:12:13:14:15:17) sts.

RIGHT FRONT
Work as for left front, working between markers for **right front** and rev all shaping.

MAKING UP
PRESS all pieces as described on the information page.
Sweater
Join right shoulder seam using back stitch.
With RS facing and using 3¹/₄mm (US 3) needles and beg at left shoulder, pick up and knit 20(20:20:20:20:22:22:22:22) sts down left front neck, knit across 13(15:15:15:17:17:19:21:21) sts on holder, pick up and knit 20(20:20:20:20:22:22:22:22) sts up right front neck and 3 sts down back neck, knit across 23(25:27:29:33:33:37:39:39) sts on holder, pick up and knit 3 sts up back neck.
(82(86:88:90:96:100:106:110:110)sts)
Work 2(2:3:3:3:3:3:3:3)cm in K2, P2 rib.
Cast off in rib.

Cardigan
Button band
With RS of left front facing for girls, right front for boys and using 3¹/₄mm (US 3) needles, pick up and knit 70(82:96:108:116:128:138:142:148) along front edge.
Work 6 rows in K2, P2 rib.
Cast off evenly in rib.
Buttonhole band
With RS of right front facing for girl, left front of boys
work as given for button band with the addition of 4(4:4:5:5:6:6:6:6) button holes worked on row 4 as folls:
Girls cardigan
Buttonhole row (RS): Rib 2, (yon, rib 2tog, rib 18(22:26:22:24:22:24:24:26)), 3(3:3:4:4:5:5:5:5) times, yon, rib 2tog, rib 6(6:8:8:8:4:4:8:4).
Boys cardigan
Buttonhole row (RS): Rib 6(6:8:8:8:4:4:8:4), (yon, rib 2tog, rib 18(22:26:22:24:22:24:24:26)), 3(3:3:4:4:5:5:5:5) times, yon, rib 2tog, rib 2.
Join both shoulder seams using back stitch.
Neckband
With RS of right front facing and using 3¹/₄ mm (US 3) needles, pick up and knit 5(5:5:5:5:7:7:7:7) sts across front band, 26(27:27:27:28:30:31:32:32) sts up right front neck, 29(31:33:35:39:39:43:45:45) sts across back neck, 26(27:27:27:28:30:31:32:32) sts down left front neck and 5(5:5:5:5:7:7:7:7) sts across front band.
(91(95:97:99:105:113:119:123:123)sts)
Work 3(3:3:3:3:3:3:3:3) rows in K2, P2 rib.
Girls cardigan
Next row (RS) buttonhole row: Rib 2, yon, rib 2tog, rib to end.
Boys cardigan
Next row (RS) buttonhole row: Rib to last 4 sts, rib 2tog, yon, rib 2.
Both girls and boys
Work 2 more rows in rib. Cast off in rib.
See information page for finishing instructions, noting that when joining sleeve seam, rev seam at cuff to allow turn back.

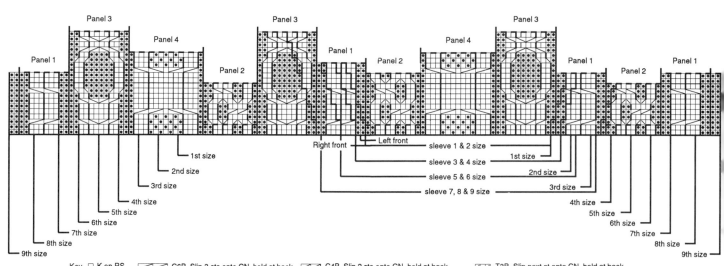

Key □ K on RS / P on WS   C6B Slip 3 sts onto CN, hold at back, K3, K3 from CN   C4B Slip 2 sts onto CN, hold at back, K2, K2 from CN   T3B Slip next st onto CN, hold at back K2, then P1 from CN

▣ P on RS / K on WS   C6F Slip 3 sts onto CN, hold at front, K3, then K3 from CN   C4F Slip 2 sts onto CN, hold at front, K2, K2 from CN   T3F Slip 2 sts onto CN, hold at front, P1, then K2 from CN

Mrs McHugh's Blanket

by LOUISA HARDING

YARN

Rowan True 4-ply Botany or Rowan 3-ply Botany

True 4-ply Botany	7	x	50gm
3ply Botany	9	x	25gm

Approximate measurement

81 x 94cm [32 x 37)ins]
(each section 17.5cm [7 ins] square)

NEEDLES

1 pair 2³/₄mm (no 12) (US 2) needles

Centre panel

SQUARE (work 12)
Cast on 55 sts using 2³/₄mm (US 2) needles.
Work 9 rows in garter st, i.e. knit every row.
Next row: K3, purl to last 3 sts, K3.
Row 1 (RS): K3, (K2tog, yo) to last 4 sts, K4.
Row 2: K3, P2, (K13, P3) twice, K13, P2, K3.
Row 3: K3, K2tog, yo, (P13, yo, sl1, K2tog, psso, yo) twice, P13, yo, K2tog, K3.
Row 4: K3, P2, (K13, P3) twice, K13, P2, K3.
Rows 5 and 7: As row 3
Rows 6 and 8: As row 4
Row 9: K3, K2tog, yo, (P6, yo, P2tog, P5, yo, sl1, K2tog, psso, yo) twice, P6, yo, P2tog, P5, yo, K2tog, K3.
Row 10: K3, P2, (K6, P1, K6, P3) twice, K6, P1, K6, P2, K3.
Row 11: K3, K2tog, yo, (P5, yo, K3tog, yo, P5, yo, sl1, K2tog, psso, yo) twice, P5, yo, k3tog, yo, P5, yo, K2tog, K3.
Row 12: K3, P2, (K5, P3, K5, P3) twice, K5, P3, K5, P2, K3.
Row 13: K3, K2tog, yo, (P4, yo, K2tog, K1, K2tog, yo, P4, yo, sl1, K2tog, psso, yo) twice, P4, yo, K2tog, K1, K2tog, yo, P4, yo, K2tog, K3.
Row 14: K3, P2, (K4, P5, K4, P3) twice, K4, P5, K4, P2, K3.
Row 15: K3, K2tog, yo, (P3, yo, K2tog, K3, K2tog, yo, P3, yo, sl1, K2tog, psso, yo) twice, P3, yo, K2tog, K3, K2tog, yo, P3, yo, K2tog, K3.
Row 16: K3, P2, (K3, P7, K3, P3) twice, K3, P7, K3, P2, K3.
Row 17: K3, K2tog, yo, (P2, yo, K2tog, K5, K2tog, yo, P2, yo, sl1, K2tog, psso, yo) twice, P2, yo, K2tog, K5, K2tog, yo, P2, yo, K2tog, K3.
Row 18: K3, P2, (K2, P9, K2, P3) twice, K2, P9, K2, P2, K3.
Row 19: As row 17
Row 20: As row 18
Row 21: K3, K2tog, yo, (P2, yo, K2tog, K2, yo, K2tog, K1, K2tog, yo, P2, yo, sl1, K2tog, psso, yo) twice, P2, yo, K2tog, K2, yo, K2tog, K1, K2tog, yo, P2, yo, K2tog, K3.
Row 22: K3, P2, (K2, P4, K1, P4, K2, P3) twice, K2, P4, K1, P4, K2, P2, K3.
Row 23: K3, K2tog, yo, (P3, yo, sl1, K2tog, psso, yo, P1, yo, K3tog, yo, P3, yo, sl1, K2tog, psso,yo) twice, P3, yo, sl1, K2tog, psso, yo, P1, yo, K3tog, yo, P3, yo, K2tog, K3.
Row 24: K3, P2, (K13, P3) twice, K13, P2, K3.
Row 25: K3, K2tog, yo, (P13, yo, sl1, K2tog, psso, yo) twice, P13, yo, K2tog, K3.
Rows 26 and 28: As row 24
Rows 27 and 29: As row 25
Row 30: K3, purl to last 3 sts, K3
Repeat from rows 1 - 30 once more
Row 61: K3, (K2tog, yo) to last 4 sts, K4.
Row 62: Knit across row.
Work 8 rows in garter st.
Cast off loosely and evenly.

MAKING UP

PRESS all pieces as described on the information page.
Using a **faggot** stitch (see diagram) sew squares together to form centre panel as foll: Join 1st, 2nd & 3rd squares together to form the width of blanket. Join 4th, 5th & 6th squares, 7th, 8th & 9th squares and 10th, 11th & 12th sqaures together in the same way.
Now join the strips together to form the centre panel.

Heart edging

Cast on 15 sts using 2 3/4mm (US 2) needles. Knit 1 row.
Row 1: (RS) K2, yo, P2tog, K2, (yo) twice, K2tog, yo, K1, yo, K2tog tbl, (yo) twice, K2, (yo) twice, K2. (21 sts)

Row 2: K3, P1, K3, P7, K4, yo, P2tog, K1. (21 sts)
Row 3: K2, yo, P2tog, K2, (yo) twice, K2tog, K2, yo, K1, yo, K2, K2tog tbl, (yo) twice, K4, (yo) twice, K2. (27 sts)
Row 4: K3, P1, K5, P11, K4, yo, P2tog, K1. (27 sts)
Row 5: K2, yo, P2tog, K2, (yo) twice, K2tog, K4, yo, K1, yo, K4, K2tog tbl, (yo) twice, K6, (yo) twice, K2. (33 sts)
Row 6: K3, P1, K7, P15, K4, yo, P2tog, K1. (33 sts)
Row 7: K2, yo, P2tog, K3, (yo) twice, K3tog tbl, K9, K3tog, (yo) twice, K11. (33 sts)
Row 8: Cast off 8 sts, K3, P13, K5, yo, P2tog, K1. (25 sts)
Row 9: K2, yo, P2tog, K4, (yo) twice, K3tog tbl, K7, K3tog, (yo) twice, K2, (yo) twice, K2. (27 sts)
Row 10: K3, P1, K3, P11, K6, yo, P2tog, K1. (27 sts)
Row 11: K2, yo, P2tog, K5, (yo) twice, K3tog tbl, K5, K3tog, (yo) twice, K5, (yo) twice, K2. (29 sts)
Row 12: K3, P1, K6, P9, K7, yo, P2tog, K1. (29 sts)
Row 13: K2, yo, P2tog, K6, (yo) twice, K3tog tbl, K3, K3tog, (yo) twice, K8, (yo) twice, K2. (31 sts)
Row 14: K3, P1, K9, P7, K8, yo, P2tog, K1. (31 sts)
Row 15: K2, yo, P2tog, K7, K3tog tbl, K4tog, pass the K3tog tbl over the K4tog, K13. (25 sts)
Row 16: Cast off 10 sts, K2, P1, K8, yo, P2tog, K1. (15 sts)
Repeating rows 1 to 16 throughout cont until edging is long enough to fit round all four sides of the centre panel.
Do not cast off.
Place work on a flat surface RS uppermost. Starting at corner, ease edging gently around corners to keep blanket flat, join edging to sides of centre panel using a **faggot** stitch, adjust length of edging if necessary.
Cast off.
Join ends of edging neatly together.
Press gently.

square 10	square 11	square 12
square 7	square 8	square 9
square 4	square 5	square 6
square 1	square 2	square 3

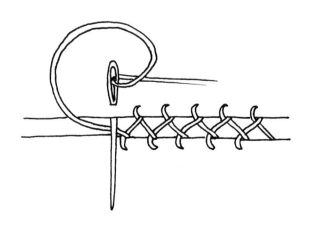

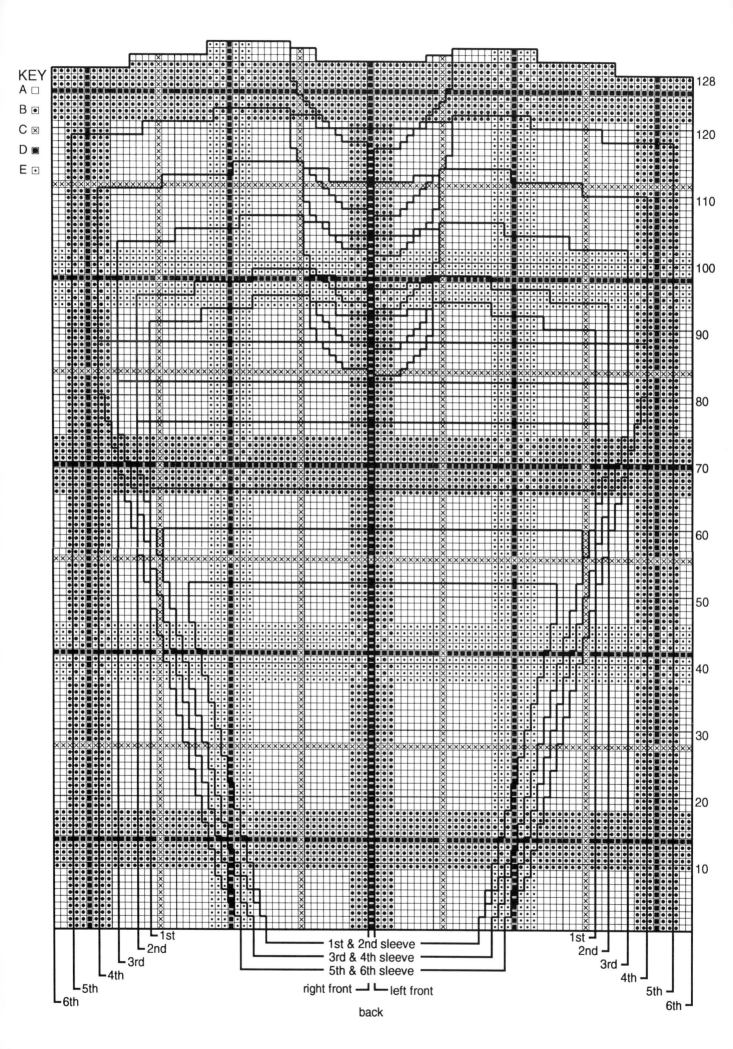

KEY
A □
B ⊡
C ☒
D ■
E ⊡

128
120
110
100
90
80
70
60
50
40
30
20
10

1st
2nd
3rd
4th
5th
6th

1st & 2nd sleeve
3rd & 4th sleeve
5th & 6th sleeve

right front — left front

back

1st
2nd
3rd
4th
5th
6th

- 62 -

Highlander

by KIM HARGREAVES

YARNS
Rowan Magpie Tweed and D.D.K

1st colourway

A	Magpie Berry	684	3(3:4:5:7:7)	100gm
B	D.D.K* Jade	661	2(3:3:3:4:4)	50gm
C	D.D.K* Grass	686	1(1:2:2:2:2)	50gm
D	D.D.K* Purple	687	1(1:2:2:2:2)	50gm
E	D.D.K* Blue	696	2(2:3:3:4:4)	50gm

2nd colourway

A	Magpie Black	62	3(3:4:5:7:7)	100gm
B	D.D.K* Pink	694	2(3:3:3:4:4)	50gm
C	D.D.K* Cream	649	1(1:2:2:2:2)	50gm
D	D.D.K* Pea	664	1(1:2:2:2:2)	50gm
E	D.D.K* Blue	665	2(2:3:3:4:4)	50gm

* used double throughout

Sizes
1st(2nd:3rd:4th:5th:6th)
2-3(3-4:4-6:6-8:8-9:9-10) yrs
Actual width
38(40.5:44:47:51.5:55)cm
[15(16:17:18¹/₂:20:21¹/₂)ins]
Length (without fringe)
39(41:44:48:51:55.5)cm
[15¹/₂(16¹/₂:17¹/₂:19:20:22)ins]
Sleeve length
25(28:30.5:35.5:38:40.5)cm
[10(11:12:14:15:16)ins]

NEEDLES
1 pair 4mm (no 8) (US 6) needles
1 pair 5mm (no 6) (US 8) needles

BUTTONS - 4(4:5:5:6:6)

TENSION
18 sts and 23 rows to 10cm measured over
patterned stocking stitch using 5mm (US 8)
needles

BACK
Cast on 69(73:79:85:93:99) sts using 5mm
(US 8) needles and yarn A.
Joining in and breaking off colours as
required cont in patt from chart for back
using the **INTARSIA** technique described on
the information page. Work until chart row
90(94:102:110:118:128) completed ending
with a WS row.
Shape shoulders and back neck
Cast off 8(9:9:10:11:12) sts at beg of next 2
rows.
Cast off 8(9:10:11:11:12) sts, patt
13(13:14:15:16:17), turn leaving rem sts on a
holder.
Work each side of neck separately.
Cast off 4 sts, patt to end.
Cast off rem 9(9:10:11:12:13) sts.
With RS facing rejoin correct yarn, cast off
centre 11(11:13:13:17:17) sts, patt to end.
Complete to match first side rev all shaping.

LEFT FRONT
Cast on 34(36:39:42:46:49) sts using 5mm
(US 8) needles and yarn A.
Joining in and breaking off colours as
required cont in patt from chart for left front
until chart row 83(87:93:101:107:117)
completed ending with a RS row.
Shape front neck
Cast off 4 sts at beg of next row.
Dec 1 st at neck edge on next 4(4:5:5:7:7)
rows and 1 foll alt row. (25(27:29:32:34:37)sts)
Cont without further shaping until front
matches back to shoulder shaping ending
with a WS row.
Shape shoulder
Keeping patt correct, cast off 8(9:9:10:11:12)
sts at beg of next row and 8(9:10:11:11:12)
sts beg foll alt row.
Work 1 row. Cast off rem 9(9:10:11:12:13) sts.

RIGHT FRONT
Work as left front, reversing all shaping and
following chart for right front.

SLEEVES (both alike)
Cast on 33(33:37:37:41:41) sts using 4mm
(US 6) needles and yarn A.
Work 6 rows in **moss st**.
Change to 5mm (US 8) needles and working
between markers for appropriate size, cont in
patt from chart for sleeve until chart row
52(60:66:76:82:88) completed, AT THE SAME
TIME shape sides by inc 1 st at each end of
3rd row and 0(5:1:1:0:3) foll alt rows and
then every foll 4th row to 57(65:69:73:79:85)
sts, ending with a WS row.
Cast off loosely and evenly.

MAKING UP
PRESS all pieces as described on the
information page.
Join both shoulder seams using back stitch.
Button band (left side girl, right side boy)
Cast on 5 sts using 4mm (US 6) needles and
work in **moss st** until band fit neatly up front
edge to beg neck shaping ending with a WS
row. Slip st into place. Cast off.
Mark position of 4(4:5:5:6:6) buttons the first
to come 1.5cm from cast on edge and last
1.5cm from neck edge and others spaced
evenly between.
Buttonhole band
Work as for button band with the addition of
4(4:5:5:6:6) buttonholes work to correspond
with button markers as folls:
Buttonhole row (RS): Patt 2, (yon) twice,
patt 2tog, patt 1.
Next row: Work across row in patt dropping
one of loops made on previous row.
Collar
Cast on 53(53:59:59:67:67) sts using 4mm
(US 6) needles.
Row 1: K2, **moss st** to last 2 sts, K2.
Row 2: Work as given for row 1.
Row 3: K2, M1, **moss st** to last 2 sts, M1, K2.
Rep these three rows until collar measures
6(6:7:8:9:10)cm from cast on edge.
Cast off in **moss st**.
See information page for finishing
instructions.
Make a fringe along bottom edge of garment,
use 4 lengths of yarn 18cm long and knot
through every 2nd st.

Mitts

YARN
One size up to 2 years knitted in Botany or
one size 2-7 years knitted in Designer D.K.
Oddments of yarn

NEEDLES
Botany
1 pair 2³/₄mm (no 12) (US 2) needles
1 pair 3¹/₄mm (no 10) (US 3) needles
Designer D.K.
1 pair 3¹/₄mm (no 10) (US 3) needles
1 pair 4mm (no 8) (US 6) needles

TENSION
28 sts and 36 rows to 10cm measured over
stocking stitch using 3¹/₄mm (US 3) needles
and **botany**, 22 sts and 28 rows to 10cm
measured over patterned stocking stitch using
4mm (US 6) needles and **Designer D.K.**

Pattern note: The pattern is written for
botany followed by Designer D.K. in **bold**.

RIGHT MITT
Cast on 37 sts using 2³/₄mm(**3¹/₄mm**) (US
2(**US 3**) needles.
Row 1 (RS): K1, (K1, P1) to last 2 sts, K2.
Row 2: K1, (P1, K1) to end.
Rep these 2 rows until work measures 5cm
from cast on edge.
Change to 3¹/₄mm(**4mm**) (US 3(**US 6**) needles
and cont in st st shaping thumb gusset as
folls: ******
Row 1 (RS)(inc): K19, P1, M1, K2, M1, P1,
K14. (39sts)
Row 2: P14, K1, P4, K1, P19.
Row 3: K19, P1, K4, P1, K14.
Row 4: Work as row 2.
Row 5 (inc): K19, P1, M1, K4, M1, P1, K14.
(41sts)
Cont inc in this manner on every 4th row
until there are 10 sts between the 2 purl sts
and ending with a RS row.
(45sts)
Work 1 row.

Work thumb
Row 1: K19, P1, K10, turn.
Row 2: P10, cast on 2sts, turn. (12sts)
Work 10 rows in st st.
Shape top
Row 1: (K2tog) to end.
Work 1 row.
Row 3: (K2tog) to end.
Break yarn, thread through sts and fasten off.
Rejoin yarn and pick up and knit 2 sts from
cast on sts at base of thumb, K to end. (37sts)
Work 16 rows in st st.
Shape top
Row 1 (RS): (K1, K2tog tbl, K13, K2tog)
twice, K1. (33sts)

Rows 2 and 4: Purl.
Row 3: (K1, K2tog tbl, K11, K2tog) twice,
K1. (29sts)
Row 5: (K1, K2tog tbl, K9, K2tog) twice, K1.
(25sts)
Row 6: Purl.
Cast off (or grafted together if preferred).

LEFT MITT
Work as given for right mitt to **.
Row 1 (RS)(inc): K14, P1, M1, K2, M1, P1,
K19. (39sts)
Row 2: P19, K1, P4, K1, P14.
Row 3: K14, P1, K4, P1, K19.
Row 4: Work as row 2.

Row 5 (inc): K14, P1, M1, K4, M1, P1, K19.
(41sts)
Cont inc in this manner on every 4th row
until there are 10 sts between the 2 purl sts
and ending with a RS row. (45sts)
Work 1 row.
Work thumb
Row 1: K14, P1, K10, cast on 2 sts, turn.
Row 2: P12, turn.
Complete to match right mitt.

MAKING UP
PRESS as described on the information page.
Join thumb and side seams using an edge to
edge stitch. Join cast off sts together.

Bobby
by LOUISA HARDING

YARN
Rowan True 4-ply Botany
2(2:3:4:5:6) 50gm
(photographed in Harebell 543 and
Snowdrop 545)

Sizes
1st(2nd:3rd:4th:5th:6th)
To fit
0mth(3mth:6-9mth:1-2:2-3:3-4)yrs
Actual width
23(27:30.5:34:37.5:41)cm
[9(10½:12:13½:14¾:16)ins]
Length
23(27:31:38:42:45)cm
[9(10½:12¼:15:16½:17¾)ins]
Sleeve length
13(16:20:23:25:28)cm
[5(6¼:8:9:10:11))ins]

NEEDLES
1 pair 2¾mm (no 12) (US 2) needles
1 pair 3¼mm (no 10) (US 3) needles

BUTTONS 3(4:4:4:5:5)

TENSION
28 sts and 36 rows to 10 cm measured over
stocking stitch using 3¼mm (US 3) needles

Moss check pattern (multiple of 10 sts plus 5)
Row 1 (RS): *(P1, K1) twice, P1, K5, rep
from * to last 5 sts, (P1, K1) twice, P1.
Row 2: *(P1, K1) twice, P1, P5, rep from * to
last 5 sts, (P1, K1) twice, P1.
Row 3, 5 & 7 (RS): Work as row 1.
Row 4 & 6: Work as row 2.
Row 8 (WS): *P5, (K1, P1) twice, K1, rep
from * to last 5 sts, P5.
Row 9: K5, (K1, P1) twice, K1, rep from * to
last 5 sts, K5.
Row 10 & 12: Work as row 8.
Row 11 & 13: Work as row 9.
Row 14: Work as row 8.
These 14 rows form the **moss check patt**.

BACK
Cast on 65(75:85:95:105:115) sts using 2¾mm
(US 2) needles and work in **moss st** as
follows:

Row 1 (RS): P1, K1, to last st P1.
Rep this row 7 times more.
Change to 3 1/4mm (US 3) needles and work
7(7:7:14:14:14) rows of **moss check patt**.
1st, 2nd & 3rd sizes only
Purl 1 row.
All sizes
Work 2 rows in st st.
Work 3 rows in **moss st**.
Rep last 5 rows once more.
Cont in st st until work measures
14(16:19:24:26:28)cm from cast on edge
ending with a WS row.
Work 3 rows in **moss st**.
Work 2 rows in st st.
Rep last 5 rows once more, ending with a
WS row. *
Work in **moss check patt** until work
measures 23(27:31:38:42:45)cm from cast on
edge, ending with a WS row.
Shape back neck
Patt 23(27:31:35:39:42) sts, turn, leave rem
sts on a holder.
Cast off 4 sts beg next row, patt to end. **
Leave rem 19(23:27:31:35:38) sts on a holder.
With RS facing slip centre
19(21:23:25:27:31) sts onto a holder, rejoin
yarn to rem sts, patt to end.
Work to match first side to **.
Work button band
Work 3 rows in **moss st**. Cast off.

FRONT
Work as for back to *.
Work in **moss check patt** until front is
14(14:16:18:18:20) rows shorter than back to
shoulder shaping.
Shape front neck
Patt 27(31:35:39:43:48) sts, turn, leave rem
sts on a holder.
Dec 1 st at neck edge on next 4(4:4:4:4:6)
rows and 4 foll alt rows.
(19(23:27:31:35:38)sts)
Work without further shaping until front
matches back to shoulder shaping ending
with a WS row. **
Work buttonhole band
Work 1 row in **moss st**.
Next row (buttonhole row): Patt
5(5:5:6:7:7:6), (yon, patt 2tog, patt

5(4:5:6:5:6) 2(3:3:3:4:4) times.
Work 1 row in **moss st**.
With RS facing slip centre centre
11(13:15:17:19:19) sts onto a holder, rejoin
yarn to rem sts, patt to end.
Work to match first side to **
Leave rem sts on a holder.

SLEEVES (both alike)
Cast on 37(37:39:45:45:51) sts using 2¾mm
(US 2) needles and work 8 rows in **moss st**
as given for back.
Change to 3¼mm (US 3) needles and cont in
st st inc 1 st at each end of 3rd row and
every foll 2nd(3rd:3rd:3rd:3rd:3rd) row to
67(67:73:81:89:101) sts and AT THE SAME
TIME, when sleeve measures
8(11:15:18:20:23)cm from cast on edge work
in patt as follows:
With RS facing and keeping inc correct work
3 rows **moss st**.
Work 2 rows st st.
Rep last 5 rows once more.
Work 7 rows in **moss check patt**.
Purl one row. Cast off evenly.

MAKING UP
PRESS all pieces as described on the
information page.
Join right shoulder by knitting sts together on
the WS.
Neckband
Using 2¾mm (US 2) needles, pick up K3 sts
from buttonhole band and
12(13:14:15:16:17) sts down left front,
K11(13:15:17:19:19) sts from holder at
centre front, pick up and
K12(:13:14:15:16:17) sts up right front and 3
sts from right back neck,
K19(21:23:25:27:31) sts from holder at
centre back, pick up and K3 sts from left
back neck and 2 sts from buttonband.
(65(69:77:83:89:95)sts)
Work 1 row in **moss st**.
Next row (RS): Patt 2, yo, Patt 2tog, patt to
end.
Work 1(1:1:1:3:3) rows in **moss st**.
Cast off in **moss st**.
See information page for finishing
instructions.

Busy Lizzy

by LOUISA HARDING

YARN

Rowan True 4-ply Botany

A Primrose	541	3(3:3:4)	50gm
B Lilac	544	1(1:1:1)	50gm
C Harebell	543	(very small amount of this)	

Sizes

1st(2nd:3rd:4th)
0-3mths(6mths:9mths:1-2yrs)

Actual width
25.5(29:33:36.5)cm
[10(11¹/₂:13:14¹/₂)ins]

Length
26(30.5:33:38)cm
[10¹/₄(12:13:15)ins]

Sleeve length
16(19:20:23)cm
[6¹/₄(7¹/₂:8:9)ins]

NEEDLES

1 pair 2³/₄mm (no 12) (US 2) needles
1 pair 3¹/₄mm (no 10) (US 3) needles

TENSION

28 sts and 36 rows to 10 cm measured over stocking stitch using 3¹/₄mm (US 3) needles

Buttons 2(2:3:3)

BACK

Cast on 72(82:92:102) sts using using 2³/₄mm (no 12) needles and yarn A and work 6 rows in **garter st** (ie. K every row).
Change to 3¹/₄mm (US 3) needles and work 2 rows in st st beg with a K row.
Joining in and breaking off colours as required, using the **fairisle technique** described on the information page and working between markers for appropriate size, work 10 rows in patt from chart.
Using yarn A cont in st st until work measures 17(19.5:21:24)cm from cast on edge ending with a RS row, inc 1 st at end of last row. (73(83:93:103)sts)
Work yoke in smocking st as folls:
Next row (foundation row) (WS): (K1,P1) to last st, K1.
Row 1 (RS): K1, (K1, P1) to last 2 sts, K2.
Row 2 and every alt row (WS): (K1, P1) to last st, K1.
Row 3 (RS): K1, (* yb, insert right hand needle from front between 3rd and 4th st on LH needle and draw through a loop, slip this loop onto LH needle and knit it together with the first st, P1, K1 *, P1) to last 4(2:4:2) sts, then work from * to * 1(0:1:0) time more, K1(2:1:2).
Row 5: Work as row 2.
Row 7: K2, P1, (* yb, insert right hand needle from front between 3rd and 4th sts on LH needle and draw through a loop, slip this loop onto LH needle and knit it together with the first st, P1, K1 *, P1) to last 2(4:2:4) sts, then work from * to * 0(1:0:1) time more, K2(1:2:1).
Row 8: As row 2.
These 8 rows form the **smocking stitch** pattern, rep the 8 rows until work measures 26(30.5:33:38) cm from cast on edge ending with a WS row.
Shape back neck
Next row (RS): Patt 23(28:33:38) sts, turn, leave rem sts on a holder.
Next row: Cast off 3 sts, patt to end.
Cast off rem 20(25:30:35)sts in rib.
With RS facing rejoin yarn to rem sts, cast off centre 27 sts, patt to end.
Complete to match first side.

LEFT FRONT

Cast on 39(44:49:54) sts using 2³/₄mm (US 2) needles and yarn A, work 6 rows in **garter st**.
Change to 3¹/₄mm (US 3) needles.
Next row (RS): Knit.
Next row: Knit 3 sts, purl to end.
Work 10 rows in fairisle pattern working between appropriate size markers for left front, AT THE SAME TIME cont to work 3 sts in garter st at front edge to form **button band**.
Using yarn A cont in st st until work measures 17(19.5:21:24)cm from cast on edge, ending with a WS row.
Next row (RS): Inc 1(0:1:0) st at beg next row patt to end. (40(44:50:54) sts)
Keeping garter st for button band correct cont in **smocking stitch** pattern as given for back, until front is 17 rows shorter than back to shoulder shaping ending with a RS row.
Shape front neck
Keeping patt correct, cast off 9(8:9:8) sts at neck edge on next row and 3 sts foll alt row. Dec 1 st at neck edge on next 4 rows and 4 foll alt rows. (20(25:30:35)sts)
Work until front matches back to shoulder.
Cast off in rib.

Mark the position of 2(2:3:3) buttons the first to come opposite start of **smocking pattern**, the last to come 1cm from neck edge rem spaced evenly between.

RIGHT FRONT

Cast on 39(44:49:54) sts using 2 3/4mm (US 2) needles and yarn A and work 6 rows in **garter st**.
Change to 3¹/₄mm (no 10) needles.
Next row (RS): Knit.
Next row (WS): Purl to last 3 sts, K3.
Complete as given for left front following chart for right front and rev all shaping and AT THE SAME TIME work buttonholes opposite button markers on left front as follows:
Buttonhole row (RS): K2tog, yon, K1, patt to end.

SLEEVES (both alike)

Cast on 37(39:39:43) sts using 2³/₄mm (US 2) needles and yarn A and work 14 rows in **smocking stitch** as for back ending with WS row.
Change to 3¹/₄mm (no 10) needles and work in stocking st until work measures 16(19:20:23)cm from cast on edge and AT THE SAME TIME inc 1 st at each end of next row and every foll 2nd(3rd:3rd:3rd) row to 67(71:73:81) sts. Cast off evenly.

MAKING UP

PRESS all pieces as described on the information page.
Join both shoulder seams using back st.
Collar
Cast on 88 sts using 2³/₄mm (US 2) needles and yarn A, work 10 rows in **garter st**.
Next row (RS): K3, M1, working between markers for collar, patt across chart row 1, M1, K3.
Next row: K3, P1, patt across chart row 2, P1, K3.
Cont working until chart row 10 completed, inc as before at each end of next row and every foll alt row to 98sts ending with a WS row. NB. Do not work any incomplete flowers.
Work 5 rows in **garter st**. Cast off knitwise.
See information page for finishing instructions.

Key □ A ▣ B ⊡ C

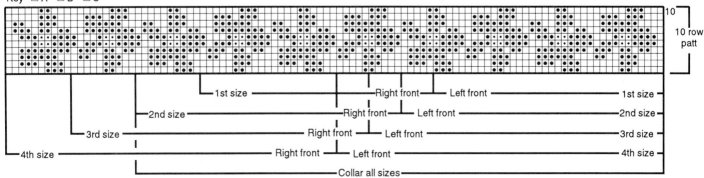

Gooseberry Hat

YARN
One size to fit up to 10 years and can be knitted in D.D.K. or Magpie Aran using oddments of yarns

NEEDLES
D.D.K
1 pair 3³/₄mm (no 10) (US 3) needles
Magpie
1 pair 4¹/₂mm (no 7) (US 7) needles

Note: The pattern is written for the D.D.K hat followed by Magpie hat in **bold**.

Hat
Cast on 106(**94**) sts using 3³/₄mm(**4¹/₂mm**) needles.
Work 8 rows in st st beg with a K row.
Row 1 (RS): K3, (P2, K2) to last 3 sts, P3.
Row 2: Work as row 1.
Rep these 2 rows twice more.

Work 16 rows in st st ending with a WS row.
Next row (RS): K1, (K2tog, K2) to last st, K1.
Work 5 rows in st st.
Next row (RS): K1, (K2tog, K1) to last st, K1.
Work 5 rows in st st.
Next row (RS): (K2tog) to end.
Work 1 row.
Next row (RS): (K2tog) to end.
Break yarn, thread through rem sts and fasten off. Join seam.

Hamish

by KIM HARGREAVES

YARNS
Rowan True 4-ply Botany

A	Primrose	541	1(1:2:2)	50gm
B	Harebell	543	1(1:1:1)	50gm
C	Spearmint	542	1(1:1:1)	50gm
D	Snowdrop	545	1(1:1:1)	50gm
E	Shell	540	1(1:1:1)	50gm

Sizes
1st(2nd:3rd:4th)
To fit
0-3(3-6:6:9)months
Actual width
25.5(29:30.5:32)cm
[10(11¹/₂:12:12¹/₂)ins]
Length
25(29:32.5:35.5)cm
[9³/₄(11¹/₂:12³/₄:14)ins]
Sleeve length
14(16.5:18:19)cm
[5¹/₂(6¹/₂:7:7¹/₂)ins]

NEEDLES
1 pair 2³/₄ (no 12) (US 2) needles
1 pair 3¹/₄mm (no 10) (US 3) needles

BUTTONS - 4

TENSION
28 sts and 36 rows to 10cm measured over patterned stocking stitch using 3¹/₄mm (US 3) needles

BACK
Cast on 71(81:85:89) sts using 2³/₄mm (US 2) needles and yarn A and work 5 rows in **moss st** as folls:
Row 1 (RS): K1, (P1, K1) to end.
Rep this row 4 times more.
Next row (WS): Purl.
Change to 3 1/4mm (US 3) needles and joining in and breaking off colours as required cont in patt from chart for back using the **INTARSIA** technique described on the information page.
Work until chart row 84(100:112:122) completed ending with a WS row.

Shape shoulders and back neck
Cast off 7(9:9:9) sts at beg of next 2 rows.
Cast off 8(9:9:10) sts, patt 12(13:14:14), turn leaving rem sts on a holder.
Work each side of neck separately.
Cast off 4 sts, patt to end.
Cast off rem 8(9:10:10) sts.
With RS facing rejoin correct yarn, cast off centre 17(19:21:23) sts, patt to end.
Complete to match first side rev all shaping.

LEFT FRONT
Cast on 40(45:47:49) sts using 2³/₄mm (US 2) needles and yarn A and work 5 rows in **moss st** as given for back.
Next row (WS): Patt 5 sts and leave these sts on a holder for front band, P to end.
(35(40:42:44)sts)
Change to 3¹/₄mm (US 3) needles and joining in and breaking off colours as required cont in patt from chart for left front until chart row 77(93:103:113) completed ending with a RS row.
Shape front neck
Cast off 4 sts at beg of next row and foll alt row.
Dec 1 st at neck edge on next 4(5:6:7) rows.
(23(27:28:29)sts)
Cont without further shaping until front matches back to shoulder shaping ending with a WS row.
Shape shoulder
Keeping patt correct, cast off 7(9:9:9) sts at beg of next row and 8(9:9:10) sts beg foll alt row. Work 1 row.
Cast off rem 8(9:10:10) sts.

RIGHT FRONT
Cast on 40(45:47:49) sts using 2³/₄mm (US 2) needles and yarn A and work 5 rows in **moss st** as given for back.
Next row (WS): Purl to the last 5 sts, turn leaving rem sts on a holder for front band.
(35(40:42:44)sts)
Change to 3¹/₄mm (US 3) needles and complete as given for left front, reversing all shaping and following chart for right front.

SLEEVES (both alike)
Cast on 37 sts using 2³/₄mm (US 2) needles and yarn A.
Work 5 rows in **moss st as** as given for back.
Next row (WS): Purl.
Change to 3¹/₄mm (US 3) needles and work 44(54:60:64) rows in patt from chart for sleeve and AT THE SAME TIME shape sides by inc 1 st at each end of 3rd row and every foll alt row to 57 sts and then every foll 4th row to 65(69:71:73) sts, ending with a WS row.
Cast off loosely and evenly.

MAKING UP
PRESS all pieces as described on the information page.
Join both shoulder seams using back stitch.
Button band (left side for girl, right side for boy)
Slip 5 sts from holder onto a 2³/₄mm (US 2) needle and keeping patt correct cont in **moss st** until band fit neatly up front edge to beg neck shaping ending with a WS row. Slip st into place.
Cast off.
Mark position of 4 buttons the first to come 8(9:10:11)cm from cast on edge and last 1.5cm from neck edge and others spaced evenly between.
Buttonhole band
Work as for button band with the addition of 4 buttonholes work to correspond with button markers as folls:
Buttonhole row (RS): Patt 2, yon patt 2tog, patt 1.
Collar
Cast on 61(65:71:73) sts using 2³/₄mm (US 2) needles.
Row 1: K3, **moss st** to last 3 sts, K3.
Row 2: Work as given for row 1.
Row 3: K3, M1, **moss st** to last 3 sts, M1, K3.
Rep these three rows until collar measures 4.5(5:5.5:6)cm from cast on edge.
Cast off in **moss st**.
See information page for finishing instructions.

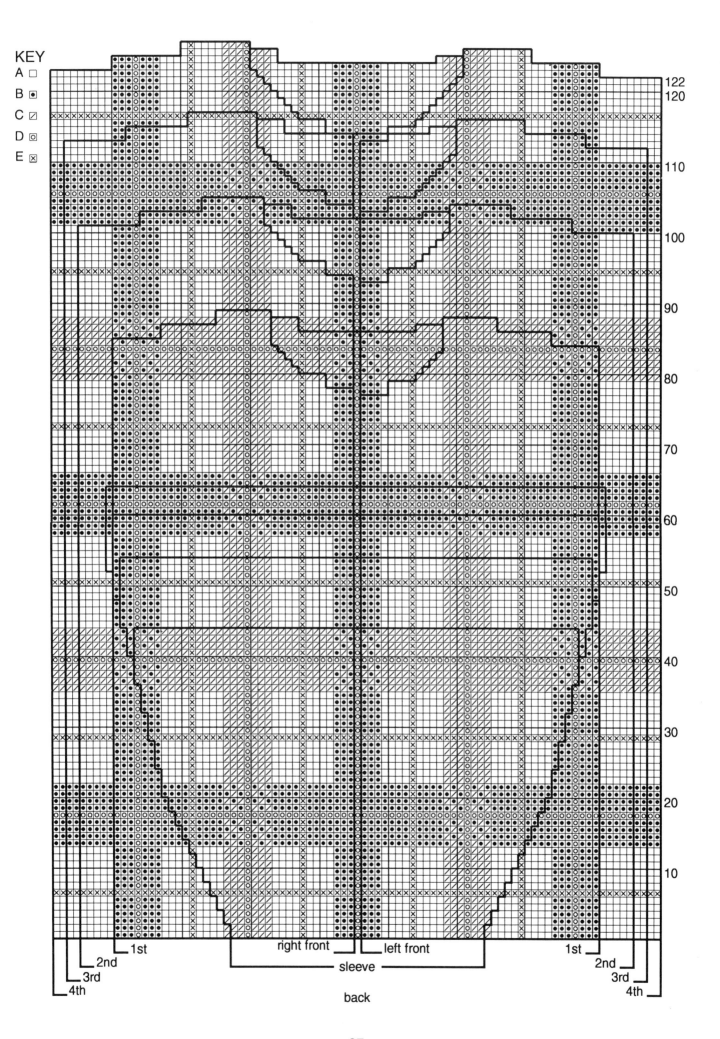

KEY
A □
B ⊡
C ▨
D ⊙
E ⊠

122
120
110
100
90
80
70
60
50
40
30
20
10

1st
2nd
3rd
4th

right front left front
sleeve
back

1st
2nd
3rd
4th

Moby

by KIM HARGREAVES

YARN
Den-m-nit
14(16:17) 50gm

Sizes
1st(2nd:3rd)
To fit
6-8(8-9:9-10)yrs
Actual width
47(51:55)cm
[18½(20:21½)ins]
Length after washing
53.5(57:61)cm
[21(22½:24)ins]
Sleeve length after washing
35.5(38:40.5)cm
[14(15:16)ins]

NEEDLES
1 pair 3¼mm (no 10) (US 3) needles
1 pair 4mm (no 8) (US 6) needles
Cable needle

TENSION
20 sts and 28 rows to 10 cm measured over
stockingstitch using 4mm (US 6) needles
before washing

BACK
Cast on 111(119:127) sts using 3¼mm (US
3) needles.
Work 22 rows from chart, beg and ending
where indicated for appropriate size and
ending with a WS row.
Change to 4mm (US 6) needles and cont
until chart row 58 completed.
Cont in patt, rep the 36 row patt as indicated

on chart until work measures
62.5(66.5:71)cm from cast on edge ending
with a WS row (this allows for shrinkage after
washing).
Shape shoulder and back neck
Cast off 12(14:15) at beg next 2 rows.
Cast off 13(14:15) patt 17(18:20), turn
leaving rem sts on a holder.
Work each side of neck separately.
Cast off 4 sts at beg next row.
Cast off rem 13(14:16) sts.
With RS facing rejoin yarn to rem sts, cast off
centre 27 sts, patt to end.
Complete to match first side revshaping.

FRONT
Work as for back until work is 14 rows
shorter than back to **shape shoulder and
back neck.**
Shape front neck
Patt 49(53:57) sts, turn, leave rem sts on a
holder.
Work each side of neck separately.
Cast off 3 sts, patt to end.
Dec 1 st at neck edge on next 5 rows and 3
foll alt rows. (38:42:46)sts)
Work without further shaping until front
matches back to shoulder shaping ending
with a WS row.
Shape shoulder
Cast off 12(14:15) sts at beg next row and
13(14:15) sts beg foll alt row.
Work 1 row.
Cast off rem 13(14:16) sts.
With RS facing rejoin yarn to rem sts, cast off
centre 13 sts, patt to end.
Complete to match first side.

SLEEVES (both alike)
Cast on 43 sts using 3¼mm (US 3) needles.
Work 22 rows in patt from chart working
between markers for sleeve.
Change to 4mm (US 6) needles and cont in
patt from chart rep the 36 row patt
throughout and AT THE SAME TIME inc 1 st
at each end of next row and 6 foll alt rows
and then every foll 4th row to 93 sts taking
extra sts into patt and as they occur and
ending with a WS row.
Cont without further shaping until sleeve
measures 41.5(44.5:47)cm from cast on edge
ending with a WS row (this allows for
shrinkage after washing).
Cast off evenly in patt.

MAKING UP
Join left shoulder seam using back stitch.
Neckband
With RS facing, using 3¼mm (US 3) needles
and beg at left shoulder, pick up and K20 sts
down left front neck, 13 sts across centre
front, 20 sts up right front neck and 35 sts
across back neck. (88sts)
Row 1 (WS): (K1, P3) to end.
Row 2: (K3, P1) to end.
Rep these 2 rows 3 times more then 1st row
once again.
Cast off in patt as set.
Join shoulder and neckband using back
stitch.
**Wash all pieces, as described on the ball
band, before sewing together.**
See information page for finishing
instructions.

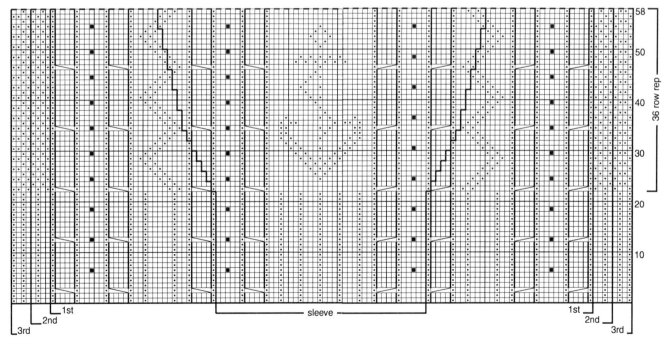

KEY
□ K on RS, P on WS
⊡ P on RS, K on WS
■ MB, Knit into the front, back,
front of next st, turn K3, turn P3,
turn K3, turn slip 1, K2tog, psso

◢ slip st 2 sts onto cable needle, hold
at back, K2, K2 from cable needle

◣ Slip next 2 sts onto cable needle, hold
at front, K2, K2 from cabe needle

Milly Mop

by KIM HARGREAVES

YARNS
Rowan True 4-ply Botany
2(3:3:3:4:5:5) 50gm
(Photographed in Shell 540 and Lilac 544)

Sizes
1st(2nd:3rd:4th:5th:6th:7th)
To fit
0mth(3mth:6mth:9mth:1-2:2-3:3-4)yrs
Actual width
23(26.5:28.5:31.5:34:38:41)cm
[9(10½:11:12½:13½:15:16)ins]
Length
22(26:29:32:35:39:41)cm
[8¾(10¼:11½:12½:13¾:15½:16)ins]
Sleeve length
13(16:19:20:23:25:28)cm
[5(6¼:7½:8:9:10:11)ins]

NEEDLES
1 pair 2¾mm (no 12) (US 2) needles
1 pair 3¼mm (no 10) (US 3) needles

BUTTONS 3(3:3:4:4:5:5)

TENSION
28 sts and 36 rows to 10cm measured over stocking stitch using 3¼mm (US 3) needles

BACK
Cast on 64(74:80:88:96:106:114) sts using 3¼mm (US 3) needles.
* Work 3 rows in st st beg with a K row.
Next row (WS): Knit.
Next row: (K2tog, yon) to last 2 sts, K2.
Next row: Knit. **
Work in st st until work measures 16(20:23:26:29:33:35)cm from cast on edge, ending with a WS row.
Shape shoulders and back neck
Cast off 7(8:9:9:11:12:13) sts,
K11(11:13:14:15:16:17), turn leaving rem sts on a holder.
Work each side of neck separately.
Cast off 4 sts, P to end.
Cast off rem 7(7:9:10:11:12:13) sts.
With RS facing rejoin yarn to rem sts, cast off centre 16(20:20:24:24:28:28) sts, K to end.
Complete to match first side reversing shaping.

LEFT FRONT
Cast on 32(37:40:44:48:53:57) sts using 3¼mm (US 3) needles.
Work as given for back from * to **.
Work in st st until front measures 6(8:9.5:12:14:16.5:18.8)cm from cast on edge ending with a WS row.
Shape front neck
Next row (RS): K to last 6 sts, K3tog tbl, K3.
Work 5 rows in st st.
Rep these last 6 rows until 20(23:26:28:32:35:39) sts rem.
Cont without further shaping until front matches back to shoulder shaping ending with a WS row.
Shape shoulder
Cast off 6(8:8:9:10:11:13) sts at beg next row and 7(8:9:9:11:12:13) sts beg foll alt row.
Work 1 row.
Cast off rem 7(7:9:10:11:12:13) sts.

RIGHT FRONT
Work as given for left front reversing shaping.

SLEEVES (both alike)
Cast on 35(35:39:39:45:49:49) sts using 2¾mm (US 2) needles and work in **moss st** as folls:
Row 1 (RS): (K1,P1) to last st K1.
Rep this row 7 times more inc 1 st at centre of last row. (36(36:40:40:46:50:50)sts)
Change to 3¼mm (US 3) needles and work as given for back from * to ** and AT THE SAME TIME inc 1 st at each end of next and every foll alt row to 62(62:62:62:56:56:56) and then for **2nd, 3rd, 4th, 5th, 6th & 7th sizes only** every foll 4th row to 70(74:78:82:86:92) sts.
(62(70:74:78:82:86:92)sts)
Cont without further shaping until sleeve measures 13(16:19:20:23:25:28)cm from cast on edge ending with a WS row.
Cast off loosely.

MAKING UP
PRESS all pieces as described on the information page.
Join both shoulder seams using back stitch.
Sew sleeves into place and join side and sleeve seams (see information page)

Lace Edging
Cast on 12 sts using 3¼mm (No 10) needles and work as folls:
Row 1 (WS): Sl 1, k3, yon, K2tog, K2, yon, K2tog, yon, K2.
Row 2: Yon, K2tog, K11.
Row 3: Sl 1, K2, (yon, K2tog) twice, K2, yon, K2tog, yon, K2.
Row 4: Yon, K2tog, K12.
Row 5: Sl 1, K3, (yon, K2tog) twice, K2, yon, K2tog, yon, K2.
Row 6: Yon, K2tog, K13.
Row 7: Sl 1, K2, (yon, K2tog) 3 times, K2, yon, K2tog, yon, K2.
Row 8: Yon, K2tog, K14.
Row 9: Sl 1, K2, (K2tog, yon) twice, K2, K2tog, (yon, K2tog) twice, K1.
Row 10: Yon, K2tog, K13.
Row 11: Sl 1, K1, (K2tog, yon) twice, K2, K2tog, (yon, K2tog) twice, K1.
Row 12: Yon, K2tog, K12.
Row 13: Sl 1, K2, K2tog, yon, K2, K2tog, (yon, K2tog) twice, K1.
Row 14: Yon, K2tog, K11.
Row 15: Sl 1, K1, K2tog, yon, K2, K2tog, (yon, K2tog) twice K1.
Row 16: Yon, K2tog, K10.
Rep these 16 rows until work edging fit around bottom of garment, leave sts on a holder. With RS out slip st edging into place around lower edge of garment, adjust length, cast off.

Front band
Cast on 5 sts using 3¼mm (US 3) needles and work in **moss st** until band fit up left front to shoulder, across back neck and down right front to beg of front neck shaping when slightly stretched. Starting at bottom of edging, slip stitch into place.
Mark position of 3(3:3:4:4:5:5) buttons the first to come 1cm above top of edging the last to come 1.5cm below front neck shaping and rem spaced evenly between.
Cont until band fits to bottom of edging working buttonholes to correspond with markers as folls:
Buttonhole row: Patt 2, yon, patt 2tog, patt 1.
Cast off and slip stitch into place.
See information page for finishing instructions.

Piper Scarf

YARN
Rowan True 4-ply Botany or D.D.K
Botany
1 x 50gm
(Photographed in Shell 540)
D.D.K
2 x 50gm

Needles
For Botany use 4mm (no 8) (US 6) needles
For D.D.K use 5mm (no 6) (US 8) needles

Cast on 26 sts using the appropriate size needles and work in patt as folls;
Row 1 (foundation row): (Yon, sl 1, K1) to end.
Row 2: (Yon, sl 1, K2tog (slipped-stitch and yon of previous row)) to end.
Rep row 2 only until work measures 66cm for botany or 91cm for D.D.K. or length required from cast on edge.
Cast off loosely.

How jacket

by KIM HARGREAVES

YARNS

Rowan Magpie Tweed and D.D.K

A	Magpie	Ocean 305	3(4:4:4)	100gm
B	D.D.K*	Black 62	6(7:8:9)	50gm
C	Magpie	Woodland 300	2(2:2:2)	100gm
D	D.D.K*	Blue 696	1(2:2:2)	50gm
E	D.D.K*	Pink 688	2(3:3:4)	50gm

* used double throughout

Sizes

1st(2nd:3rd:4th)
3-4(5-6:7-8:9-10) yrs
Actual width
40.5(44:47:50.5)cm
[16(17:18 1/2:20)ins]
Length
46(50.5:55:60)cm
[18(20:21 1/2:23 1/2)ins]
Sleeve length
28(30.5:35.5:38.5)cm
[11(12:14:15)ins]

NEEDLES

1 pair 4mm (no 8) (US 6) needles
1 pair 5mm (no 6) (US 8) needles

BUTTONS - 4(4:5:5)

TENSION

18 sts and 23 rows to 10cm measured over
patterned stocking stitch using 5mm (US 8)
needles

BACK

Cast on 73(79:85:91) sts using 4mm (US 6)
needles and yarn A and work 6 rows in st st
beg with a K row.
Next row (RS): Purl to form foldline.
Next row (WS): Purl.
Change to 5mm (US 8) needles and joining
in and breaking off colours as required cont
in patt from chart for back using the
INTARSIA technique described on the
information page.
Work until chart row 106(116:126:136)
completed ending with a WS row.
Shape shoulders and back neck
Cast off 8(9:9:10) sts at beg of next 2 rows.
Cast off 9(10:10:11) sts, patt 13(14:14:15),
turn leaving rem sts on a holder.
Work each side of neck separately.
Cast off 4 sts, patt to end.
Cast off rem 9(10:10:11) sts.
With RS facing rejoin correct yarn, cast off
centre 13(13:19:19) sts, patt to end.
Complete to match first side rev all shaping.

POCKET LININGS 3rd & 4th sizes only

(make 2)
Cast 19 sts using 5mm (US 8) needles and
work 24 rows in st st beg with a K row.
Leave sts on a holder.

LEFT FRONT

Cast on 33(36:39:42) sts using 4mm (US 6)
needles and yarn A and work 6 rows in st st
beg with a K row.
Next row (RS): Purl to form hemline, turn

and cast on 13 sts. (46(49:52:55)sts)
Next row (WS): Purl.
Change to 5mm (US 8) needles and joining
in and breaking off colours as required cont
in patt from chart for left front until chart row
74(74:38:38) completed ending with a WS
row.

3rd & 4th size only
Place pocket
Chart row 39 (RS): Patt 10(13), slip next 19
sts onto a holder, patt across sts of first
pocket lining, patt to end.
Cont until chart row 82(82) completed.

All sizes
Shape front neck
Next row (RS): Patt to the last 10 sts, turn
and leave these 10 sts on a holder for collar.
Cont working from chart dec 1 st at neck
edge on 3rd row and every foll 3rd row to
26(29:29:32) sts.
Cont without further shaping until front
matches back to shoulder shaping ending
with a WS row.
Shape shoulder
Keeping patt correct, cast off 8(9:9:10) sts at
beg of next row and 9(10:10:11) sts beg foll
alt row.
Work 1 row. Cast off rem 9(10:10:11) sts.

RIGHT FRONT

Cast on 33(36:39:42) sts using 5mm (US 8)
needles and yarn A and work 6 rows in st st
beg with a K row.
Next row (RS): Purl to
form hemline.
Next row: Purl, to end,
turn and cast on 13 sts.
(46(49:52:55)sts)
Change to 5mm (US 8)
needles and complete as
given for left front
following chart for right
front and reversing all
shaping, placing of pocket
on 3rd and 4th sizes and
making buttonholes as
indicated, working
buttonhole rows as folls:
Buttonhole row (RS):
(Patt 3, yon twice, patt
2tog) twice, patt to end.
Next row: Patt across row
dropping one of loops
made at each buttonhole
on previous row.

SLEEVES (both alike)

Cast on 35(35:39:39) sts
using 4mm (US 6) needles
and yarn A.
Work 6 rows in st st beg
with a K row.
Next row (RS): Purl to
form foldline.
Next row: Purl.
Change to 5mm (US 8)
needles and working
between markers for

appropriate size, cont in patt from chart for
sleeve until chart row 64(70:82:88)
completed, and AT THE SAME TIME shape
sides by inc 1 st at each end of 9th row and
8 foll alt rows and then every foll 4th row to
69(69:83:83) sts, ending with a WS row. Cast
off loosely and evenly.

MAKING UP

PRESS all pieces as described on the
information page.
Join both shoulder seams using back stitch.
Pocket tops
With RS facing and using 4mm (US 6)
needles, slip stitches from holder onto LH
needle.
Work 3 rows in patt from chart.
Using yarn A, P2 rows.
Work 4 rows in st st. Cast off.
Collar (both sides alike)
With RS facing slip sts from holder onto a
5mm (US 8) needle and work 50(60:72:82)
rows in patt from chart for collar and AT THE
SAME TIME inc 1 st at each end of 3rd row
and every foll alt row to 44(44:52:52) sts.
Cast off.
Join cast off edges of collar together using
back stitch. Sew collar neatly into place
matching centre of collar to centre of back
neck. Fold collar and front band in half and
slip stitch into place on WS.
Slip stitch bottom edges of bands together.
See info page for finishing instructions.

COLLAR

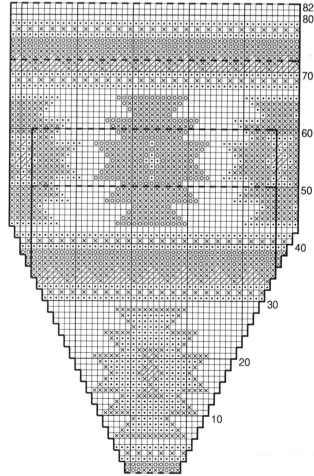

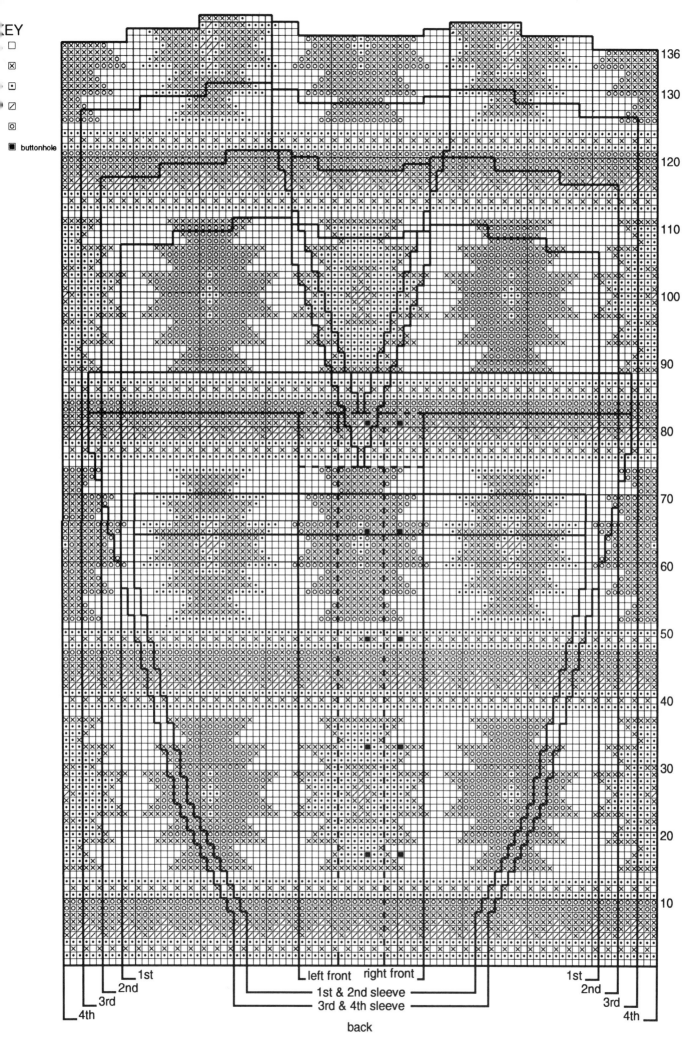

KEY

□
☒
·
▨
◎
■ buttonhole

left front   right front

1st
2nd
3rd
4th

1st & 2nd sleeve
3rd & 4th sleeve

1st
2nd
3rd
4th

back

- 71 -

Bonnie Hat

by Kim Hargreaves

Yarn
Rowan Designer D.K.
Colourway 1
A   Sky   655   1 x 50gm
Small amount of B Salmon 689, C Lime 664,
D Sage 690 and E Rust 663
Colourway 2
A   Natural 649   1 x 50gm
Small amount of B Navy 671, C Rose 70, D
Maroon 659 and E Grass 660

Needles
1 pair 3¹/₄mm (no 10)(US 3) needles
1 pair 4mm (no 8)(US 6) needles
Hat
Cast on 131 sts using 3¹/₄mm (US 3) needles
and yarn A and work 14 rows in K1, P1 rib,

inc 1 st at end of last row. (132 sts)
Next row (RS): Change to 4mm (No 8)
needles and work 4 rows in st st ending with
a WS row.
Work 15 rows in **fairisle** patt from chart rep
the 12 st rep 11 times across row ending with
a RS row.
Work 3 rows in st st.
Shape crown
Row 1 (RS) (dec): K2, (K2tog, K8), rep to
end. (119 sts)
Row 2 and every WS row: Purl.
Row 3 (dec): K2, (K2tog, K7), rep to end.
(106 sts)
Row 5 (dec): K2, (K2tog, K6), rep to end.
(93 sts)
Cont dec in this way working 1 st less

between dec on every RS row until 28 sts
rem, ending with a WS row.
Next row (RS)(dec): K2, (K2tog), rep to end.
(15 sts)
Break yarn and draw up the 15 sts and fasten
off. Join seam.

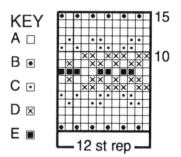

Sampler

by KIM HARGREAVES

YARNS
Rowan Magpie and Designer D.K.

A	Magpie	Raven	62		
	or Porridge	771	4(4:5:7:8)	100gm	
B	D.D.K *	664	1(1:1:1:1)	50gm	
C	D.D.K *	65	1(1:1:2:2)	50gm	
D	D.D.K *	685	1(1:1:2:2)	50gm	
E	D.D.K *	694	1(1:1:2:2)	50gm	
F	D.D.K *	659	1(1:1:2:2)	50gm	
G	D.D.K *	665	1(1:2:2:2)	50gm	

* All D.D.K yarns used double throughout.
(5th size photographed in Raven 62, 3rd size
photographed in Porridge 771)

Sizes
1st(2nd:3rd:4th:5th)
To fit
3-4(4-6:6-8:8-9:9-10) yrs
Actual width
40.5(44:47:50.5:55)cm
[16(17:18¹/₂:20:21 1/2)ins]
Length
45(49.5:53.5:57:61)cm
[17¹/₂(19¹/₂:21:22¹/₂:24)ins]
Sleeve length
28(30.5:35.5:38:41)cm
[11(12:14:15:16)ins]

NEEDLES
1 pair 4mm (no 8) (US 6) needles
1 pair 5mm (no 6) (US 8) needles

TENSION
18 sts and 23 rows to 10cm measured over
patterned stocking stitch using 5mm (US 8)
needles

BACK
Cast on 72(78:84:90:98) sts using 4mm (US

6) needles and yarn A.
Work 2.5cm in K2, P2 rib ending with a WS
row and inc 1 st at end of last row
(73(79:85:91:99)sts).
Change to 5mm (US 8) needles, and joining
in and breaking off colours as required and
using mixture of **fairisle** and **intarsia**
technique described on the information page
cont in patt from chart for back until chart
row 98(108:118:126:134) completed ending
with a WS row.
Shape shoulders and back neck
Cast off 7(8:9:9:11) sts at beg of next 2 rows.
Cast off 7(8:9:10:11) sts, patt
12(12:13:14:15), turn leaving rem sts on a
holder.
Work each side of neck separately.
Cast off 4 sts, work to end.
Cast off rem 8(8:9:10:11) sts.
With RS facing rejoin appropriate yarns to
rem sts, cast off centre 21(23:23:25:25) sts,
work to end.
Complete to match first side.

FRONT
Work as for back until chart row
90(100:110:118:124) completed ending with
a WS row.
Shape front neck
Patt 30(33:36:39:43) sts, turn leaving rem sts
on a holder.
Work each side of neck separately.
Cast off 3(3:3:4:4) sts at beg next row.
Dec 1 st at neck edge on next 4(5:5:4:4)
rows and 1(1:1:2:2) foll alt rows.
(22(24:27:29:33)sts)
Cont without further shaping until front
matches back to shoulder shaping ending
with a WS row.
Shape shoulder
Cast off 7(8:9:9:11) sts at beg next row and

7(8:9:10:11) sts beg foll alt row.
Work 1 row.
Cast off rem 8(8:9:10:11) sts.
With RS facing appropriate yarns to rem sts,
cast off centre 13 sts, work to end.
Complete as for first side reversing shaping.

SLEEVES (both alike)
Cast on 36(36:40:40:40) sts using 4mm (US
6) needles and yarn A.
Work 2.5cm in K2, P2 rib ending with a WS
row and inc 1 st at end of last row.
(37(37:41:41:41)sts)
Change to 5mm (US 8) needles and working
between appropriate markers, cont in patt
from chart until chart row 58(64:76:82:88)
completed and AT THE SAME TIME shape
sides by inc 1 st at each end of 3rd row and
every foll 3rd row to 69(73:71:71:71)sts and
then for **3 largest sizes only** every 4th row to
79(83:85) sts, ending with a WS row.
(69(73:79:83:85)sts)
Cast off loosely and evenly.

MAKING UP
PRESS all pieces as described on the
information page.
Join right shoulder seam using back stitch.
Neck band
With RS facing using 4mm (US 6) needles
and yarn A pick up and knit 14(14:14:15:16)
sts down left front neck, 13 sts across centre
front, 14(14:14:15:16) sts up right front neck
and 29(31:31:33:33) sts across back neck.
(70(72:72:76:78)sts)
Work 5 rows in K2, P2 rib.
Cast off loosely and evenly in rib.
See information page for finishing
instructions.

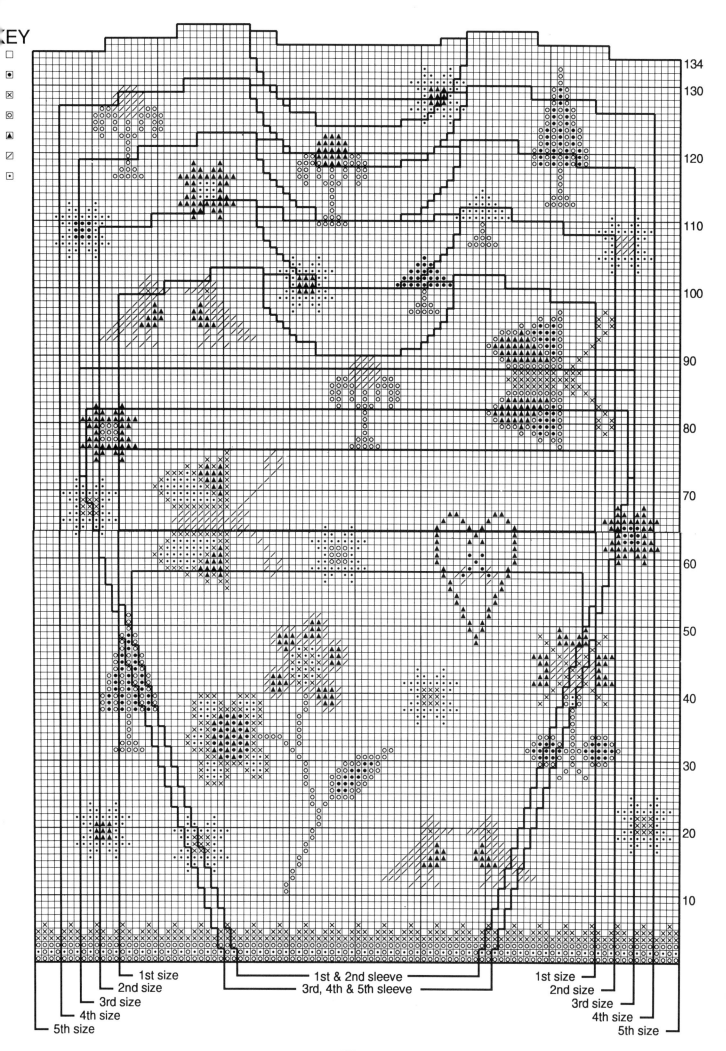

KEY

□
•
⊠
◉
▲
⁄
·

134
130
120
110
100
90
80
70
60
50
40
30
20
10

1st size
2nd size
3rd size
4th size
5th size

1st & 2nd sleeve
3rd, 4th & 5th sleeve

1st size
2nd size
3rd size
4th size
5th size

Nann

by KIM HARGREAVES

YARNS

Rowan D.D.K

A Cream	649	2(2:2:3:3:3:3:4:4)	50gm
B Black	62	1(1:1:1:1:1:1:2:2)	50gm
C Blue	665	3(3:4:5:5:5:6:6:7)	50gm

Sizes

1st(2nd:3rd:4th:5th:6th:7th:8th:9th)
To fit
6mth(9mth:1-2:2-3:3-4:4-6:6-8:8-9:9-10)yrs
Actual width
29(32:35.5:38:41:43.5:47:51:55.5)cm
[11¹/₂(12¹/₂:14:15:16:17:18¹/₂:20:22)ins]
Length
31(34:39:43:46:51:55:58:62)cm
[12¹/₄(13¹/₂:15¹/₂:17:20:21¹/₂:23:24¹/₂)ins]
Sleeve length
19(20:23:25:28:30.5:35.5:38:40.5)cm
[7¹/₂(8¹/₂:9:10:11:12:14:15:16)ins]

NEEDLES

1 pair 3¹/₄mm (no 10) (US 3) needles
1 pair 4mm (no 8) (US 6) needles

BUTTONS - 4(4:4:5:5:5:6:6:6)

TENSION

22 sts and 30 rows to 10cm measured over
stocking stitch, 24 sts and 27 rows to 10cm
measured over fairisle, using 4mm (US 6)
needles

LEFT FRONT

Cast on 32(36:40:42:44:48:52:56:60) sts
using 3¹/₄mm (US 3) needles and yarn A and
work 12 rows in **basket st** as folls:
Rows 1 & 3 (RS): K0(4:0:2:4:0:4:0:4), (P4,
K4) to end.
Rows 2 & 4: (P4, K4) to last
0(4:0:2:4:0:4:0:4) sts, P0(4:0:2:4:0:4:0:4).
Rows 5 & 7: P0(4:0:2:4:0:4:0:4), (K4, P4) to
end.
Rows 6 & 8: (K4, P4) to last
0(4:0:2:4:0:4:0:4) sts, K0(4:0:2:4:0:4:0:4).
Work first 4 rows once more, **dec** 1 st at end
of last row on **2nd and 3rd** sizes and **inc** 1 st
at end of last row on **5th and 9th** sizes.
(32(35:39:42:45:48:52:56:61)sts)
Change to 4mm (US 6) needles and cont in st
st beg with a K row until work measures
17(18.5:22:23.5:25:28:30:32:34)cm from
cast on edge ending with a RS row.
Next row (WS)(inc): Purl across row inc
3(3:3:3:4:4:4:5:5) sts evenly across row.
(35(38:42:45:49:52:56:61:66)sts)
Join in yarn B and work 32 rows in patt from
chart A working between markers for
appropriate size, ending with a WS row.
Cont from chart rep row 29 to 32 throughout
until work measures
27(30:35:39:41.5:46.5:50:52:56)cm from
cast on edge ending with a RS row.
Shape front neck
Cast off 5(5:5:5:5:5:6:6:6) sts at beg of next
row and 2(2:2:2:3:3:3:3:4) beg foll alt row.
Dec 1 st at neck edge on next
4(4:5:5:5:5:5:6:8) rows.
(24(27:30:33:36:39:42:46:48)sts)

Cont without shaping until work measures
31(34:39:43:46:51:55:58:62)cm from cast on
edge ending with a WS row.
Shape shoulder
Cast off 8(9:10:11:12:13:14:15:16) sts at beg
next row and foll alt row.
Work 1 row.
Cast off rem 8(9:10:11:12:13:14:16:16) sts.

RIGHT FRONT

Cast on 32(36:40:42:44:48:52:56:60) sts
using 3¹/₄mm (US 3) needles and yarn A and
work 12 rows in **basket st** as folls:
Rows 1 & 3 (RS): (K4, P4) to last
0(4:0:2:4:0:4:0:4) sts, K0(4:0:2:4:0:4:0:4).
Rows 2 & 4: P(4:0:2:4:0:4:0:4) sts, (K4, P4)
to end.
Rows 5 & 7: (P4, K4) to last
0(4:0:2:4:0:4:0:4) sts, P0(4:0:2:4:0:4:0:4).
Rows 6 & 8: K0(4:0:2:4:0:4:0:4) sts, (K4, P4)
to end.
Work first 4 rows once more, **dec** 1 st at end
of last row on **2nd and 3rd** sizes and inc 1 st
at beg of last row on **5th and 9th** sizes.
(32(35:39:42:45:48:52:56:61)sts)
Complete as for left front reversing shaping
and following chart for right front.

KEY

A □
B ☒
C ☑

BACK

Cast on 64(68:76:84:88:96:104:112:120sts
using 3¹/₄mm (US 3) needles and yarn C.
Work 12 rows in **basket st** as folls:
Rows 1 & 3 (RS): (K4, P4) to last
0(4:4:4:0:0:0:0:0) sts, K0(4:4:4:0:0:0:0:0).
Rows 2 & 4: P0(4:4:4:0:0:0:0:0), (K4, P4) to
end.
Rows 5 & 7: (K4, P4) to last
0(4:4:4:0:0:0:0:0) sts, P0(4:4:4:0:0:0:0:0).
Rows 6 & 8: (P4, K4) to last 4 sts, P4.
Work first 4 rows once more inc 1 st at each
end of last row on **2nd, 3rd, 5th & 9th** sizes.
(64(70:78:84:90:96:104:112:122)sts)
Change to 4mm (US 6) needles and cont in st
st beg with a K row until back measures
same as fronts to shoulder shaping ending
with a WS row.
Shape shoulders and back neck
Cast off 7(8:9:10:11:12:13:14:15) sts at beg
of next 2 rows.
Cast off 7(8:9:10:11:12:13:14:15) sts, patt
11(12:13:14:14:15:16:17:19) turn leaving
rem sts on a holder.
Work each side of neck separately.
Cast off 3 sts, work to end.
Cast off rem 8(9:10:11:11:12:13:14:16) sts.

Chart B

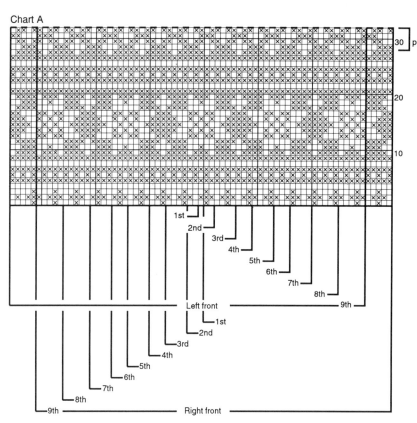

Chart A

- 74 -

With RS facing rejoin yarn, cast off centre 14(14:16:16:18:18:20:22:24) sts and work to end.
Complete to match first side rev shaping.

SLEEVES (both alike)
Cast on 33(33:37:37:41:41:47:47:47) sts using 3¹/₄mm (US 3) needles and yarn C and work 4 rows in **moss st** as folls:
Row 1 (RS): K1, (P1, K1) to end.
Rep this row 3 times more.
Change to 4mm (US 6) needles.
Joining in yarns B and A work 6 rows in patt from chart B and AT THE SAME TIME inc 1 st at each end of 3rd row.
(35(35:39:39:43:43:49:49:49)sts)
Using yarn C throughout cont in st st inc 1 st at each end of next row and every foll 4th row to 55(57:63:69:67:67:91:95:101)sts and then for **5th and 6th sizes only** every foll 3rd row to 79(83) sts.
(55(57:63:69:79:83:91:95:101)sts)
Cont without further shaping until sleeve

measures 19(20:23:25:28:30.5:35.5:38:40.5) cm or length required from cast on edge ending with a WS row.
Cast off loosely and evenly.

MAKING UP
PRESS all pieces as described on the information page.
Join both shoulder seams using back stitch.
Button band (left side for girl, right side for boy)
Cast on 7 sts using 3¹/₄mm (US 3) needles and yarn A, work in **moss st** until band fit neatly up front edge to beg neck shaping slip st into place. Cast off.
Mark position of 4(4:4:5:5:5:6:6:6) buttons the first to come 6cm from cast on edge and last 1.5cm from neck edge and rem spaced evenly between.
Buttonhole band
Work as for button band with the addition of 4(4:4:5:5:5:6:6:6) buttonholes worked to correspond with markers as folls:

Buttonhole row (RS): Patt 3, (yon) twice, patt 2tog, patt 2.
Next row: Work across row in patt dropping one of loops made on previous row.
Collar
Cast on 57(57:59:61:69:69:77:79:81) sts using 3¹/₄mm (US 3) needles and yarn A.
Row 1: K3, work in **moss st** to last 3 sts, K3.
Row 2: Work as row 1.
Row 3 (inc): K3, M1, working **moss st** to last 3 sts, M1, K3.
Rep these 3 rows until work measures 6(6.5:7:7:7.5:7.5:8:8.5:9) cm from cast on edge.
Cast off in patt.
Starting and ending halfway across front bands and matching centre of collar with centre back neck, slip stitch cast on edge of collar into place.
See information page for finishing instructions leaving 5cm open at lower side seam to form vents.

Sailor Sam
by KIM HARGREAVES

YARN
Rowan Den-m-nit and Handknit D.K. cotton

A	Den-m-nit	225	8(9:9:10:11)	50gm
B	True Navy	244	4(4:5:6:6)	50gm

Sizes
1st(2nd:3rd:4th:5th)
To fit
3-4(4-6:6-8:8-9:9-10) yrs
Actual width
41(44:47:51:55)cm
[16(17¹/₄:18¹/₂:20:21 1/2)ins]
Length after washing
45(49.5:53.5:57:61)cm
[17³/₄(19¹/₂:21:22¹/₂:24)ins]
Sleeve length after washing
28(30.5:35.5:38:40.5)cm
[11(12:14:15:16)ins]

NEEDLES
1 pair 3¹/₄mm (no 10) (US 3) needles
1 pair 4mm (no 8) (US 6) needles

TENSION
20 sts and 29 rows to 10 cm measured over pattern using 4mm (US 6) needles before washing

BACK
Cast on 82(90:94:102:110) using 3¹/₄mm (US 3) needles and yarn A and work 8 rows in **garter st** ie knit every row.
Change to 4mm (US 6) needles.
Row 1 (RS): K2, (P2, K2) to end.
Row 2: P2, (K2, P2) to end.
Rep these 2 rows twice more and 1st row once more.
Next row (WS): Purl across row dec 2 sts over row on **2nd size only**.
(82(88:94:102:110)sts)
Join in yarn B and work in striped patt as folls:

Row 1 (RS): K using yarn B.
Row 2: P using yarn B.
Rows 3 & 5: K using yarn A.
Rows 4 & 6: P using yarn A.
These 6 rows form the patt and are repeated throughout.
Rep these 6 rows until work measures 52(56.5:61.5:65:69.5)cm from cast on edge ending with a WS row (this allows for shrinkage after washing).
Shape shoulder and back neck
Patt 29(32:34:37:41) turn, leave rem sts on a holder.
Work each side of neck separately.
Cast off 4 sts, patt to end.
(25(28:30:33:37)sts)
Leave sts on a holder.
With RS facing rejoin yarn and cast off centre 24(24:26:28:28) sts, K to end.
Complete to match first side.

FRONT
Work as for back until work is 16(18:20:22:22) rows shorter than back to shape shoulder and back neck.
Shape front neck
Patt 36(39:42:46:50) sts, turn, leave rem sts on a holder.
Work each side of neck separately.
Cast off 3 sts, patt to end.
Dec 1 st at neck edge on next 7(6:6:5:5) rows and 1(2:3:5:5) foll alt rows.
(25(28:30:33:37)sts)
Work without further shaping until front matches back to shoulder shaping ending with a WS row.
Leave sts on a holder.
With RS facing rejoin yarn to rem sts, cast off centre 10 sts, patt to end.
Complete to match first side.

SLEEVES (both alike)
Cast on 42(42:46:46:46) using 3¹/₄mm (US 3) needles and yarn A, work 6 rows in **garter st**.
Row 1 (RS): K2, (P2, K2) to end.
Row 2: P2, (K2, P2) to end.
Rep these 2 rows once more and then 1st row again.
Next row: Purl.
Change to 4mm (US 6) needles and joining in yarn B cont in striped patt as given for back and AT THE SAME TIME inc 1 st at each end of next row and every foll 4th row to 72(76:68:74:76) sts and then for **3rd, 4th & 5th sizes only** every foll 6th row to 82(86:92). (72(76:82:86:92)sts)
Cont without further shaping until sleeve measures 31(34:40:43:45.5)cm from cast on edge ending with a WS row (this allows for shrinkage after washing). Cast off loosely.

MAKING UP
Join left shoulder seam by casting off sts together on RS.
Neckband
With RS facing, using 3¹/₄mm (US 3) needles and yarn A and beg at left shoulder, pick up and K18(19:22:24:24) sts down left front neck, 10 sts across centre front, 18(19:22:24:24) sts up right front neck and 32(32:34:36:36) sts across back neck.
(78(80:88:94:94)sts)
Work 6 rows in K2, P2 rib.
Work 6 rows in st st beg with P row.
Cast off loosely and evenly.
Join right shoulder seam as for left shoulder seam, join neck band seam with back stitch, rev seam over st st so that it curls onto RS.
Wash all pieces, as described on the ball band, before sewing together.
See information page for finishing instructions.

Pie Man

by KIM HARGREAVES

YARN
Rowan Magpie Aran
6(7:8:9:10) 100gm
(Photographed in Berry 684)

Sizes
1st(2nd:3rd:4th:5th)
To fit
3-4(4-6:6-8:8-9:9-10) yrs
Actual width
41(44:47:51:55)cm
[16(17^1/$_4$:18^1/$_2$:20:21 1/2)ins]
Length
45(49.5:53.5:57:61)cm
[18(19^1/$_2$:21:22^1/$_2$:24)ins]
Sleeve length
31.5(34:39:41.5:44)cm
[12^1/$_2$(13^1/$_2$:15^1/$_2$:16^1/$_2$:17^1/$_2$)ins]

NEEDLES
1 pair 4mm (no 8)(US 6) needles
1 pair 5mm (no 6) (US 8) needles
Cable needle

TENSION
18 sts and 23 rows to 10cm measured over
stocking stitch using 5mm (US 8) needles

BACK
Cast on 74(80:84:92:100) sts using 4mm (US
6) needles.
Row 1 (RS): P0(1:0:0:0), K0(2:1:1:1), (P2, K2)
to last 2(1:3:3:3) sts, P2(1:2:2:2), K0(0:1:1:1).
Row 2: K0(1:0:0:0), P0(2:1:1:1), (K2, P2) to
last 2(1:3:3:3:3) sts, K2(1:2:2:2), P0(0:1:1:1).
Rep these 2 rows 3 times more and then 1st
row once again.
Next row (WS)(inc): Rib 6(9:11:15:19), *
(M1, rib 2), twice, (rib 2, M1) 4 times, rib 4,

M1, rib 2, M1 *, rib 4, (rib 2, M1) 8 times,
rib 6, rep from * to * once more, rib to end.
(98(104:108:116:124)sts)
Change to 5mm (US 8) needles and cont in
patt from chart for back working between
appropriate markers and placing the panels
as indicated. Rep the patts throughout cont
until work measures 45(49.5:53.5:57:61)cm
from cast on edge ending with a WS row.
Shape shoulders and back neck
Cast off 10(11:11:12:13)sts at beg next 2 rows.
Cast off 10(11:11:12:14) patt 15(16:16:17:18)
sts, turn leaving rem sts on a holder.
Work each side of neck separately.
Cast off 4 sts, patt to end.
Cast off rem 11(12:12:13:14) sts.
With RS facing rejoin yarn to rem sts, off
centre 28(28:32:34:34) sts pattern to end.
Complete to match first side reversing all
shaping.

FRONT
Work as for back until front is 10(10:12:12:12)
rows shorter than back to shape shoulder
ending with a WS row.
Shape front neck
Patt 41(44:44:47:51)sts, turn leaving rem sts
on a holder.
Work each side of neck separately.
Cast off 4 sts patt to end.
Dec 1 st at neck edge on next 5 rows and 1
foll alt row. (31(34:34:37:41)sts)
Cont without further shaping until front
matches back to shoulder shaping ending
with a WS row.
Shape shoulder
Cast off 10(11:11:12:13)sts at beg next row
and 10(11:11:12:14) beg foll alt row.
Work 1 row.
Cast off rem 11(12:12:13:14) sts.
With RS facing rejoin yarn to rem sts cast off

SLEEVE

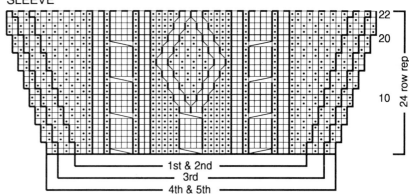

back & front

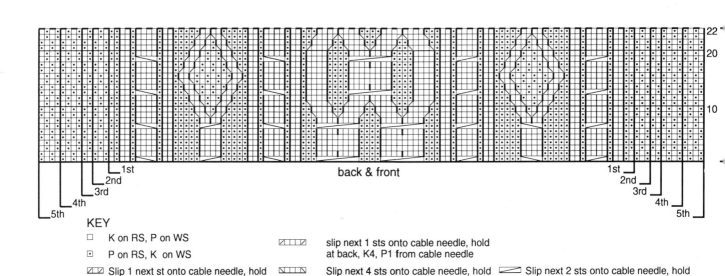

KEY

☐   K on RS, P on WS

⊡   P on RS, K on WS

Slip 1 next st onto cable needle, hold
at back, K2, P1 from cable needle

Slip next 2 sts onto cable needle, hold
at front, P1, K2 from cable needle

slip next 1 sts onto cable needle, hold
at back, K4, P1 from cable needle

Slip next 4 sts onto cable needle, hold
at front, P1, K4 from cable needle

Slip next 4 sts onto cable needle, hold
at back, K4, K4 from cable needle

Slip next 2 sts onto cable needle, hold
at back, K2, K2 from cable needle

Slip next 2 sts onto cable needle, hold
at front, K2, K2 from cable needle

centre 16(16:20:22:22) sts patt to end.
Complete as for first side reversing shaping.

SLEEVES (both alike)
Cast on 32(32:38:42:42) sts using 4mm (US 6) needles.
Row 1 (RS): K1(1:0:2:2), (P2, K2) to last 3(3:2:0:0) sts, P2(2:2:0:0) sts, K1(1:0:0:0).
Row 2: P1(1:0:2:2), (K2, P2) to last 3(3:2:0:0) sts, K2(2:2:0:0) sts, P1(1:0:0:0).
Rep these 2 rows 3 times more then 1st row once more.
Next row (WS)(inc): Rib 7(7:10:12:12), * M1, rib 2, M1, rib 4, (M1, rib 2) twice *, rep

from * to * once more, rib to end.
(40(40:46:50:50)sts)
Change to 5mm (US 8) needles and cont in patt from chart for sleeve working between appropriate markers, placing the panels as indicated and rep the patts throughout shape sides by inc 1 st at each end of 3rd row and every foll 3rd row to 66(66:60:60:60) sts and then every foll 4th row to 74(78:84:88:94) sts taking extra sts into double moss st.
Cont without further shaping until sleeve measures 31.5(34:39:41.5:44)cm or length required from cast on edge.
Cast off in patt.

MAKING UP
PRESS all pieces as described on the information page.
Join right shoulder seam using back stitch.
With RS facing and using 4mm (US 6) needles and beg at left shoulder, pick up and knit 17(17:19:19:19) sts down left front neck, 16(16:20:22:22) sts across centre front, 17(17:19:19:19) sts up right front neck and 36(36:40:42:42) sts across back neck.
(86:86:98:102:102)sts)
Work 12(12:12:13:13)cm in K2, P2 rib.
Cast off in rib.
See info page for finishing instructions.

$Pee\ Wee$

by KIM HARGREAVES

YARNS
Rowan Magpie
3(4:4:5:5:6:7:7:8) 100gm
(Photographed in natural 002)
Sizes
1st(2nd:3rd:4th:5th:6th:7th:8th:9th)
6mth(9mth:1-2:2-3:3-4:4-6:6-8:8-9:9-10) yrs
Actual width
29(32.5:35:37.5:41:44:47.5:51:55)cm
[11^1/$_2$(12^3/$_4$:13^3/$_4$:15:16:17^1/$_4$:18^1/$_2$:20:21^1/$_2$)ins]
Length
30.5(33:38:42:45:49.5:53.5:57:61)cm
[12(13:15:16^1/$_2$:18:19^1/$_2$:21:22^1/$_2$:24)ins]
Sleeve length
21(22:25.5:27.5:31.5:34:39:42.5:45)
[8^1/$_4$(8^3/$_4$:10:11:12^1/$_2$:13^1/$_2$:15^1/$_2$:16^3/$_4$:17^3/$_4$)ins]

NEEDLES
1 pair 4mm (no 8) (US 6) needles
1 pair 4^1/$_2$mm (no 7) (US 7) needles

BUTTONS (1st, 2nd & 3rd sizes only) - 3

TENSION
18 sts and 23 rows to 10cm measured over reversed stocking stitch using 4^1/$_2$mm (US 7) needles

BACK
Cast on 52(58:64:68:74:80:86:92:100) sts using 4mm (US 6) needles.
Work 4(4:4:4:6:6:6:6:6) row in **garter stitch** ie knit every row.
Change to 4^1/$_2$mm (US 7) needles, cont in **reversed st st** beg with a **purl** row, until work measures 30.5(33:38:42:45:49.5:53.5:57:61)cm from cast on edge ending with a WS row.
Shape shoulders and back neck
1st, 2nd & 3rd sizes only
Next row (RS): Purl 15(17:19) sts and leave these on a holder for shoulder, P22(24:26) sts leave these on a holder for back neck, P to end.
Work 2 rows more in **reversed st st** to form band for shoulder buttons.
Cast off.
4th, 5th, 6th, 7th, 8th & 9th sizes only
Next row (RS): Purl 25(27:30:32:34:38),

turn leaving rem sts on a holder.
Work each side of neck separately.
Cast off 4 sts, K to end.
(21:23:26:28:30:34)sts)
Leave rem sts on a holder.
Return to rem sts, with RS facing slip centre 18(20:20:22:24:24) sts onto a holder, rejoin yarn and purl to end.
Complete to match first side.

FRONT
Work as for back until front is 8(8:10:10:10:10:10:12:12) rows shorter than back to shoulder shaping ending with a WS row.
Shape front neck
Purl 19(21:25:27:29:32:34:36:40) sts, turn leaving rem sts on a holder.
Work each side of neck separately.
Dec 1 st at neck edge on next 4(4:6:6:6:6:6:6:6) rows.
(15(17:19:21:23:26:28:30:34)sts)
Cont without further shaping until front matches back to shoulder ending with a WS row.*
4th, 5th, 6th, 7th, 8th & 9th sizes only
Leave rem sts on a holder.
1st, 2nd & 3rd sizes only
Work buttonhole band for shoulder fastening
Purl 2 rows.
Buttonhole row (RS): P2, yon, P2tog, P4(6:7), yon, P2tog, P to end.
Purl 1 row.
Cast off.
All sizes
Return to rem sts and with RS facing slip centre 14(16:14:14:16:16:18:20:20) sts onto a holder, rejoin yarn and purl to end.
Work as for first side to *.
Leave rem sts on a holder.

SLEEVES (both alike)
Cast on 30(30:32:32:36:36:42:42:42) sts using 4^1/$_2$mm (US 7) needles.
Work 12(12:12:12:14:14:16:18:18) rows in **reversed st** beg with a purl row and ending with a WS row.
Inc 1 st at each end of next and every

foll 4th row to 46(48:52:58:66:70:74:78:84) sts.
Cont without further shaping until sleeves measures 21(22:25.5:27.5:31.5:34:39:42.5:45)cm from cast on edge ending with a WS row.
Cast off loosely.

MAKING UP
PRESS all pieces except ribbing on wrong side using a warm iron over a damp cloth.
Join right shoulder by casting off sts together on RS.
Neckband
With RS facing and using 4mm (US 6) needles and beg at left shoulder, on **first 3 sizes only** pick up and knit 2 sts across buttonhole band, pick up and knit 8(8:10:10:10:10:10:12:12) sts down left front neck, knit across 14(16:14:14:16:16:18:20:20) sts from holder at centre front, pick up and K8(8:10:10:10:10:10:12:12) sts up right front neck and 0(0:0:4:4:4:4:4:4) sts from side back neck, knit across 22(24:26:18:20:20:22:24:24) sts from holder at centre back and pick up and knit 0(0:0:4:4:4:4:4:4) sts up side back neck, on **first 3 sizes only** pick up and knit 2 sts from button band.
(56(60:64:60:64:64:68:76:76)sts)
4th, 5th, 6th, 7th, 8th & 9th sizes only
Work 4(6:6:6:6:6) rows in st st beg with a **purl** row.
Cast off loosely purlwise.
Join left shoulder seam as for right shoulder seam.
Join neck band so the when band rolls over onto the right side the seam does not show.
1st, 2nd & 3rd sizes only
Purl 1 row.
Next row (buttonhole row) (RS): K1, P2tog, yon, K to end.
Work 2 rows in st st beg with a P row.
Cast off loosely purlwise.
Join back and front at left shoulder edge overlapping front onto back.
Sew on buttons.
See information page for finishing instructions.

Fisherman sweater

by KIM HARGREAVES

YARNS
Rowan Handknit D.K. cotton
7(8:10:10:13:14:16) 50gm
(Photographed in 255 Scarlet)

Sizes
1st(2nd:3rd:4th:5th:6th:7th)
1-2(2-3:3-4:4-6:6-8:8-9:9-10)yrs
Actual width
35(38:41:44:47:51:56)cm
[13³/₄(15:16:17¹/₄:18¹/₂:20:21¹/₂)ins]
Length
38(42:45:49.5:53.5:57:61)cm
[15(16¹/₂:18:19¹/₂:21:22¹/₂:24)ins]
Sleeve length
23(28:30.5:35.5:38:40.5)cm
[9(10:11:12:14:15:16)ins]

NEEDLES
1 pair 3¹/₄mm (no 10) (US 3) needles
1 pair 4mm (no 8) (US 6) needles

TENSION
20 sts and 28 rows to 10cm measured over
stocking stitch using 4mm (US 6) needles

BACK
Cast on 71(77:83:89:95:103:111) sts using
3¹/₄mm (US 3) needles.
Work 6 rows in **garter st** ie knit evert riw.
Change to 4mm (US 6) needles and work
rows 5 to 16 from chart for **lower border
back** as folls:

Next row (RS): K4, beg and ending where
indicated, work row 5 of chart for **lower
border back**, rep the 6 st patt
10(10:12:12:14:14:17) times across row until
4 sts rem, K4.
Next row: K4, work row 6 from chart for
lower border back to last 4 sts, K4.
Knitting first and last 4 sts on every row, cont
until chart row 16 completed ending with a
WS row.
Beg with a K row cont in st st across all sts
until work measures
19(21.5:22:25.5:28:30.5:33)cm from cast on
edge ending with a WS row.
Work first 15 rows of patt from chart for **back
upper border**, beg and ending where
indicated, working 6 st patt
11(12:13:14:15:16:18) times across row and
ending with a RS row.
Next row (WS)(inc):
K13(16:19:22:25:29:33), (M1, K1) 5 times,
K3, (M1, K1) 3 times, K24, (M1, K1) 3 times,
K3, (M1, K1) 5 times, K to end.
(87(93:99:105:111:119:127)sts)
Cont in patt from chart for **yoke** until chart
row 40(44:50:54:58:60:64) completed
ending with a WS row.
Shape shoulders and back neck
Cast off 9(10:10:11:11:13:14) sts at beg next
row.
Cast off 9(10:11:12:12:13:14) sts, patt
13(14:15:16:16:17:19), turn leaving rem sts
on a holder.

Work each side of neck separately.
Cast off 4 sts, patt to end.
Cast off rem 9(10:11:12:12:13:15) sts.
With RS facing rejoin yarn to rem sts, cast off
centre 25(25:27:27:33:33:33) sts, patt to end.
Complete to match first side.

FRONT
Work as for back until row
32(36:40:44:48:50:52) of chart for **yoke**
completed ending with a WS row.
Shape front neck
Patt 36(39:41:44:46:50:54) sts, turn leave
rem sts on a holder.
Work each side of neck separately.
Cast off 4 sts, patt to end.
Dec 1 st at neck edge on next 5(5:5:5:7:7:7)
rows. (27(30:32:35:35:39:43)sts)
Cont without further shaping until front
matches back to shoulder shaping ending
with a WS row.
Shape shoulder
Cast off 9(10:10:11:11:13:14) sts at beg next
row and 9(10:11:12:12:13:14) beg foll alt
row.
Work 1 row.
Cast off rem 9(10:11:12:12:13:15) sts.
With RS facing rejoin yarn to rem sts, cast off
centre 15(15:17:17:19:19:19) sts patt to end.
Complete as for first side reversing shaping.

SLEEVES (both alike)
Cast on 34(34:38:38:44:44:44) sts using

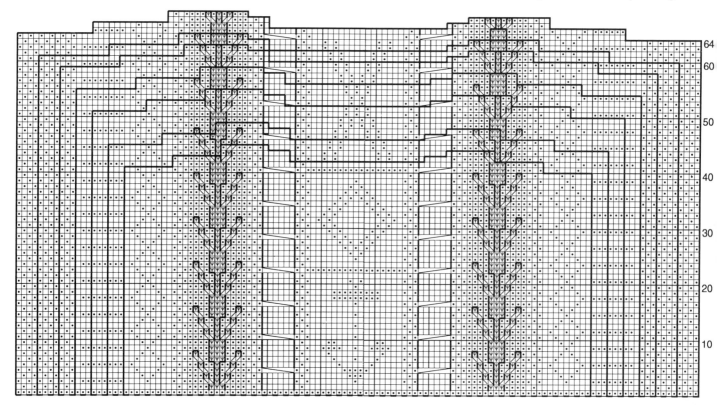

KEY
☐ K on RS, P on WS
⊡ P on RS, K on WS

ⱳ Knit into back of stitch on RS rows
　 Purl into back of stitch on WS rows

⧄ Slip next st onto cable needle hold
　 at back, K1, P1 from cable needle

⧅ Slip next st onto cable needle hold
　 at front, P1, K1 from cable needle

▱ Slip next 3 sts onto cable needle hold
　 at back, K3, K3 from cable needle

▱ Slip next 3 sts onto cabel needle hold
　 at front, K3, K3 from cable needle

Upper border
back/front

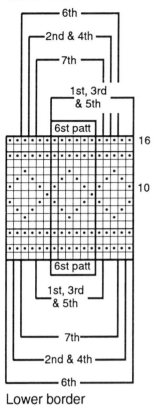

Lower border
back/front

Upper border
sleeve

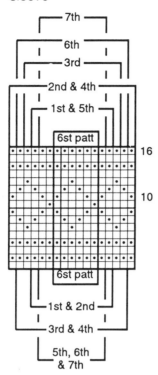

Lower border
sleeve

$3^{1}/_{4}$mm (US 3) needles and work 2.5cm in K2, P2 rib ending with a WS row and inc 1 st at end of last row.
(35(35:39:39:45:45:45)sts)
Change to 4mm (US 6) needles.
Work 16 rows in patt from chart for **lower border sleeve** and AT THE SAME TIME inc 1 st at each end of 3rd row and 4 foll 3rd rows ending with a WS row.
(45(45:49:49:55:55:55)sts)
Cont in st st beg with a K row, inc every 3rd(3rd:3rd:3rd:4th:4th:3rd) row to 59(65:73:77:83:87:67)sts and then for **largest size only** every foll 4th row to 93sts.
(59(65:73:77:83:87:93)sts)
Cont without further shaping until sleeve measures 18(20:23:25.5:30.5:33:35.5)cm from cast on edge ending with a WS row.
Work 16 rows in patt from chart for **upper border sleeve**.
Work 2 rows in st st.
Cast off loosely and evenly.

MAKING UP
PRESS all pieces as described on the information page.
Join right shoulder seam using back stitch.
Neck band
With RS facing, using $3^{1}/_{4}$mm (US 3) needles, beg at left shoulder, pick up and knit 12(12:15:15:15:15:15) sts down left front neck, 15(15:17:17:17:17:17) sts across centre front, 12(12:15:15:15:15:15) sts up right front neck and 33(33:35:35:41:41:41) sts across back neck. (72(72:82:82:88:88:88)sts)
Work 6 rows in K2, P2 rib.
Cast off in rib.
See information page for finishing instructions.

McTavish

by LOUISA HARDING

YARN
Rowan Magpie or Magpie Natural
5(6:6:8:10) 100gm
(Photographed in Dolphin 770 and Woodland 300)

Sizes
1st(2nd:3rd:4th:5th)
To fit
2-3(4-5:6-7:8-9:9-10)yrs
Actual width
39(43:47.5:51.5:55.5)cm
[15$^{1}/_{2}$(17:18$^{3}/_{4}$:20:22)ins]
Length
45(49.5:53.5:57:61)cm
[18(19$^{1}/_{2}$:21:22$^{1}/_{2}$:24)ins]
Sleeve length
28(30.5:35.5:38:40.5)cm
[11(12:14:15:16)ins]

NEEDLES
1 pair 5mm (no 6) (US 8) needles
1 pair 6mm (no 4) (US 10) needles
Cable needle

BUTTONS 5(5:6:6:7) buttons

TENSION
19 sts and 21 rows measured over cable pattern using 6mm (US 10) needles

BACK
Cast on 73(81:89:97:105) sts using 6mm (US 10) needles and work bottom band in fabric st as follows:
Row 1 (RS): Sl 1, (yarn forward, sl 1 purlwise, yarn back, K1) to end.
Row 2: Sl 1, P1, (yarn back, sl 1 purlwise, yarn forward, P1) to last st, K1.
These 2 rows form the **fabric stitch**.
Rep these 2 rows 4 times more, inc 1 st at end of last row. (74(82:90:98:106)sts)
Set sts for cable patt and side vents as folls:
Row 1 (RS): Work 6 sts in fabric st, P3, beg and ending where indicated work across chart row 1 of cable patt, rep the 8st rep 6(7:8:9:10) times across row, 9 sts rem, P3, work 6 sts in **fabric st**.
Row 2: Work 6 sts in **fabric st**, K3, work

across chart row 2, to last 9 sts, K3, work 6 sts in **fabric st**.
Keeping patt correct, cont as set until chart row 26 completed ending with a WS row.
This completes the side vents
Keeping cable patt correct and rep the 24 row patt throughout (as indicated on chart) cont as folls:
Next row (RS): P9, work in patt from chart to last 9 sts, P9.
Next row: K9, work in patt from chart to last 9 sts, K9.
Cont in patt as set, keeping 9 sts either side in **rev st st** until work measures 32(34.5:37:39.5:42) cm from cast on edge ending with a RS row and dec 1 st at end of last row. (73(81:89:97:105)sts)
Commence yoke
Cont to work in **Fabric st** (as given for border) until work measures 45(49.5:53.5:57:61)cm from cast on edge ending with a WS row.
Shape shoulders and back neck
Next row (RS): Keeping **fabric st** correct,

cast off 7(8:10:10:12)sts at beg next 2 rows.
Cast off 8(9:10:11:12)sts, patt 11(12:12:14:15) sts, turn leaving rem sts on a holder.
Work each side of neck separately.
Cast off 3 sts, patt to end.
Cast off rem 8(9:9:11:12) sts.
With RS facing rejoin yarn to rem sts, cast off centre 21(23:25:27:27) sts patt to end.
Complete to match first side rev all shaping.

POCKET LININGS (Work 2)
Cast on 14(16:18:18:20) sts using 5mm (US 8) needles.
Work 23 rows in st st beg with a K row.
Row 24 (WS): inc 4 sts evenly across row.
(18(20:22:22:24)sts) Leave sts on a holder.

LEFT FRONT
Cast on 35(39:43:47:51) sts using 6mm (US 10) needles and work 10 rows in **fabric st** as given for back.
Set sts for cable patt and side vents as folls:
Next row (RS): Work 6 sts in **fabric st**, P3, beg and ending where indicated work across chart row 1 of cable patt, rep the 8st patt 2(2:3:3:4) times across row, P2(6:2:6:2) sts.
Next row: K2(6:2:6:2) sts, work across chart row 2, to last 9 sts, K3, work 6 sts in **fabric st**.
Keeping patt correct cont until chart row 24 completed.
Place pocket
Row 25 (RS): Work 6 sts in fabric st, patt 6(7:8:8:10) sts, slip next 18(20:22:22:24) sts onto a holder and patt across 18(20:22:22:24) sts from pocket lining, patt to end.
Work 1 row. This completes the side vent.
Keeping patt correct and working the side sts in reversed st st as on back, cont until front matches back to **commence yoke** ending with a WS row.
Cont to work in **Fabric st** until work measures 40(44.5:48:51:54) cm from cast on edge ending with a RS row.
Shape neck
Next row (WS): Cast off 5(5:5:6:6) sts beg next row, patt to end.
Dec 1 st at neck edge on next 5 rows and 2(3:4:4:4) foll alt rows. (23(26:29:32:36)sts)
Cont without further shaping until matches back to beg shoulder shaping ending with a WS row.

Shape shoulders
Cast off 7(8:10:10:12) sts beg next row and 8(9:10:11:12) beg foll alt row.
Work 1 row. Cast off rem 8(9:9:11:12) sts.

RIGHT FRONT
Work as given for left front reversing all shaping and position of pocket.

SLEEVES (both alike)
Cast on 31(31:39:47:47) sts using 6mm (US 10) needles and work 10 rows in **fabric st** as given for back, inc 1 st on last row.
(32(32:40:48:48)sts)
Set stitches for cable pattern as folls:
Chart row 1 (RS): Beg and ending where indicated work chart row 1 of cable patt, rep the 8st patt 3(3:4:5:5) times across row.
Keeping cable patt correct and repeating the 24 row patt throughout cont until work measures 28(30.5:35.5:38:40.5)cm, or length required, from cast on edge and AT THE SAME TIME shape sides by inc 1 st at each end of 3rd row and every foll 3rd(3rd:4th:4th:4th) row to 62(66:70:74:80) sts taking the extra stitches into reversed stocking stitch as they occur. Cast off evenly.

MAKING UP
PRESS all pieces as described on the information page.
Pocket tops
With RS facing usin 6mm (US 10) needles slip sts from holder onto LH needle.
Work 3 rows in **fabric st**.
Cast off evenly in patt.
Button band
With RS of left front for girl and right front for boy and using 6mm (US 10) needles pick and knit 87(95:103:111:117)sts across front edge.
Work 9 rows in **fabric st**. *
Cast off in patt.
Buttonloop band
With RS of right front for girl and left front for boy work as for button band to *.
Next row (RS): Cast off 3 sts in patt for **boys jacket**, cast off 10(10:9:12:12) sts in patt for **girls jacket**, * patt 2 (3 sts on RH needle), turn and using a spare needle cont on these 3 sts only, work 14 more rows in patt, ending with a RS row. With RS of garment facing,

twist loop forward so that RS of loop faces RS of garment and needles are parallel, taking one st from loop and 1 st from band together cast off 3 sts, (1 loop completed). Cast off 11(13:11:12:10) sts, rep from * 3(3:4:4:5) times more, work 1 more button loop.
Cast off rem sts.
Join both shoulder seams using backstitch.
Collar
Cast on 65(67:69:73:73) sts using 6mm (US 10) needles and work 10 rows in **fabric st**.
Next row inc (RS): K1, M1, Patt to last st, M1, K1.
Work 3 rows in patt.
Rep these 4 rows until collar measures 7(8:9:10:10)cm. Cast off evenly in patt.
Match centre of cast on edge of collar to centre back neck, slip stitch collar into place starting and ending halfway across front bands.
See information page for finishing instructions.

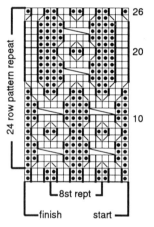

Key
☐ K on RS, P on WS

◨ P on RS, K on WS

T3F Slip 2 sts onto CN, hold at front, P1 K2 from CN

T3B Slip next st onto CN, hold at back, K2, P1 from CN

C4F Slip 2 sts onto CN, hold at front, K2, K2 from CN

Jelly Hat
by KIM HARGREAVES

YARN
Rowan True 4-ply Botany
One size up to 9 months 1 x 50g
Rowan D.D.K or Magpie
One size up to 10 years   1 x 50gm D.D.K or
                          1 x 100gm Magpie

NEEDLES
Botany
1 pair 2³/₄mm (no 12) (US 2) needles
1 pair 3¹/₄mm (no 10) (US 3) needles
D.D.K
1 pair 3¹/₄mm (no 10) (US 4) needles
1 pair 4mm (no 8) (US 6) needles

Magpie
1 pair 4mm (no 8) (US 6) needles
1 pair 5mm (no 6) (US 8) needles

Hat
Cast on 96 sts using the smaller size needle appropriate to yarn used.
Work 8 rows in K1, P1 rib.
Change to larger size needle needles.
Row 1 (RS): (P3, K3) to end.
Row 2: Work as row 1.
These 2 rows form the rib patt and are rep throughout. Cont until work measures 15cm for **botany** or 22cm for **D.D.K or Magpie** or

length required, ending with a WS row.
Shape crown
Row 1 (RS): (P3tog, K3) to end. (64sts)
Row 2: (P3, K1) to end.
Row 3: (P1, K3) to end.
Rep last 2 rows once more and then 2nd row again.
Next row: (P1, K3tog) to end. (32sts)
Work 3 rows in K1, P1 rib.
Next row: K2tog to end.
Break yarn leaving approximately 50cm length. Thread yarn through sts, pull up tight and fasten off. Join seam.

Hearts and Flowers

by KIM HARGREAVES

YARNS
Rowan Designer D.K.

A Ecru	649	5(6:6:7:9:10)	50gm
B Pink	694	1(1:1:1:1:2)	50gm
C Steel	65	1(1:1:1:1:1)	50gm
D Duckegg	665	1(1:1:1:1:1)	50gm
E Green	685	1(:1:1:1:1:1)	50gm
F Navy	671	1(1:1:1:1:1)	50gm
G Port	663	1(1:1:1:1:1)	50gm
H Sand	693	1(1:1:2:2:2)	50gm

Sizes
1st(2nd:3rd:4th:5th:6th)
9-12mth(1-2:3-4:5-7:8-9:9-10)yrs
Actual width
31(36:41:46:51:56)cm
[12(14:16:18:20:22)ins]
Length
31.5(38.5:45:51.5:56.5:61)cm
12^1/$_2$(15:17^1/$_2$:20:22:24)ins]
Sleeve length
20(23:27.5:33.5:38:41)cm
[8(9:10:13:15:16)ins]

NEEDLES
1 pair 3^1/$_4$mm (no 10) (US 3) needles
1 pair 4mm (no 8) (US 6) needles

TENSION
24 sts and 31 rows to 10cm measured over pattern using 4mm (US 6) needles

Pattern note: Do not work **any part Heart motifs** at the sides, top of back, front or sleeves, work all these stitches in background colour.

BACK
Cast on 75(87:99:111:123:135) sts using 3^1/$_4$mm (US 3) needles and yarn A.
Work 8 rows in **moss stitch** from chart.

Change to 4mm (US 6) needles, and joining in and breaking of colours as required and using the **intarsia and fairisle** techniques described on the information page cont in patt from chart for back until chart row 98(120:140:160:176:190) completed ending with a WS row.

Shape shoulders and back neck
Cast off 6(8:10:12:13:15) sts at beg of next 2 rows.
Cast off 7(8:10:12:14:16) sts, knit 11(13:15:16:18:20), turn leaving rem sts on a holder.
Work each side of neck separately.
Cast off 4 sts, work to end.
Cast off rem 7(9:11:12:14:16) sts.
With RS facing slip centre 27(29:29:31:33:33) sts onto a holder, rejoin yarn and work to end.
Complete to match first side.

FRONT
Work as for back until chart row 86(108:128:148:162:176) completed ending with a WS row.

Shape front neck
Knit 32(38:44:49:55:61) sts, turn leaving rem sts on a holder.
Work each side of neck separately.
Cast off 3 sts at beg next row and foll alt row.
Dec 1 st at neck edge on next 6(7:7:7:8:8) rows. (20(25:31:36:41:47)sts)
Cont without further shaping until front matches back to shoulder shaping ending with a WS row.

Shape shoulder
Cast off 6(8:10:12:13:15) sts at beg next row and 7(8:10:12:14:16) sts beg foll alt row.
Work 1 row.
Cast off rem 7(9:11:12:14:16) sts.
With RS facing slip centre 11(11:11:13:13:13) sts onto a holder, rejoin yarn and work to end.
Complete as for first side reversing shaping.

SLEEVES (both alike)
Cast on 35(35:41:41:51:51) sts using 3^1/$_4$mm (US 3) needles and yarn A and working between appropriate markers cont in patt from chart for sleeve.
Work 8 rows in **moss st** from chart.
Change to 4mm (US 6) needles and cont until chart row 62(72:86:104:118:128) completed and AT THE SAME TIME shape sides by inc 1 st at each end of next row and every foll 3rd row to 45(61:87:99:69:69) sts and then every foll 4th(4th:0:0:4th:4th) row to 63(71:87:99:103:111) sts, ending with a WS row.
Cast off loosely and evenly.

MAKING UP
PRESS all pieces as described on the information page.
Join right shoulder seam using back stitch.
Neck band
With RS facing, using 3^1/$_4$mm (US 3) needles and yarn A, beg at left shoulder, pick up and knit 19(19:19:19:21:21) sts down left front neck, knit across 11(11:11:13:13:13) sts at centre front, pick up and knit 19(19:19:19:21:21) sts up right front neck, and 4 sts down right back neck, knit across 27(29:29:31:33:33) sts from holder at back neck, pick up and knit 4 sts up left back neck. (84(86:86:90:96:96)sts)
Work 6 rows in **moss st**.
Cast off evenly in pattern.
Join left shoulder seam using back stitch and neck band using edge to edge st.
See information page for finishing instructions.

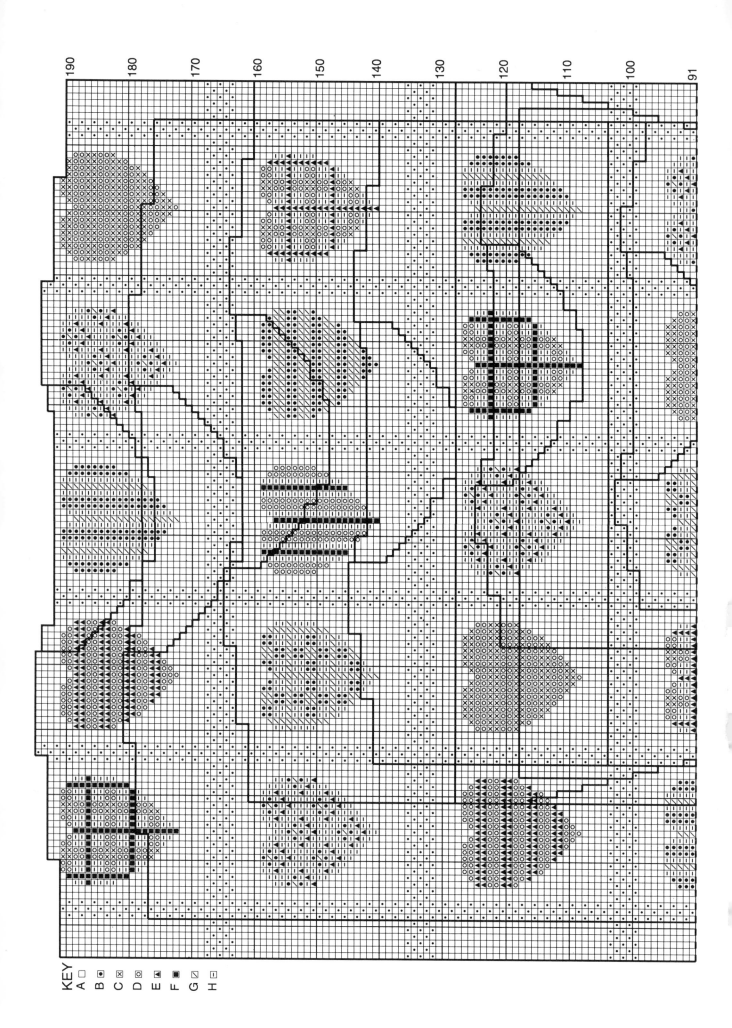

KEY
A □
B ▣
C ⊠
D ⊡
E ◀
F ■
G ◫
H ⊡

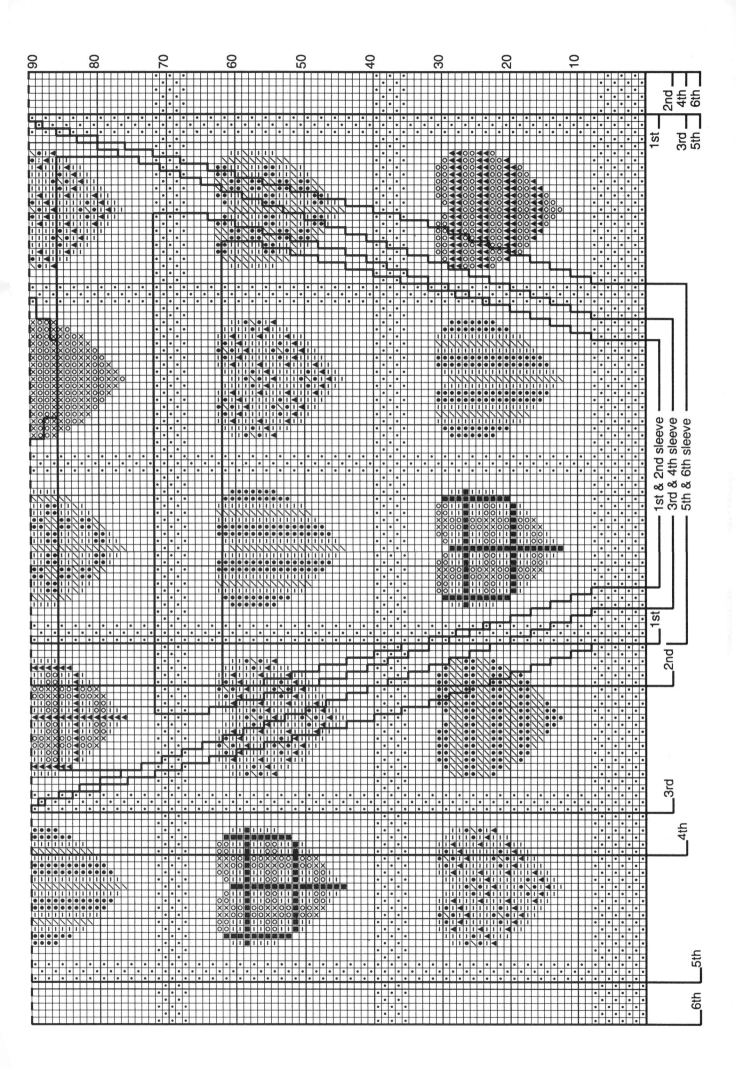

Mary Mary

by KIM HARGREAVES

YARNS
Rowan Handknit D.K. cotton
5(5:6:6:8:9:10:13:14) 50gm
(Photographed in 239 Icewater and 229 Popcorn)

Sizes
1st(2nd:3rd:4th:5th:6th:7th:8th:9th)
To fit
6mth(9mth:1-2:2-3:3-4:4-6:6-8:8-9:9-10) yrs
Actual width
26.5(29.5:32.5:35.5:36.5:39.5:42.5:46.5:50.5)cm
[10^1/$_2$(11^3/$_4$:12^3/$_4$:14:14^1/$_2$:15^1/$_2$:16^3/$_4$:18^1/$_4$:20)ins]
Length
26(28:31:32:35.5:38.5:42:47.5:51)cm
[10^1/$_4$(11:12^1/$_4$:12^3/$_4$:14:15:16^1/$_2$:18^1/$_2$:20)ins]
Sleeve length
22(23.5:26.5:30:32:34:39:42:44)cm
[8^3/$_4$(9:10^1/$_2$:11^3/$_4$:12^1/$_2$:13^1/$_2$:15^1/$_2$:16^1/$_2$:17^1/$_2$)ins]

NEEDLES
1 pair 3^1/$_4$mm (no 10) (US 3) needles
1 pair 4mm (no 8) (US 6) needles

BUTTONS 4(4:4:4:5:5:5:6:6)

TENSION
20 sts and 28 rows to 10cm measured over stocking stitch using 4mm (US 6) needles

BACK
Cast on 53(59:65:71:73:79:85:93:101) sts using 4mm (US 6) needles.
Work 7(9:11:11:13.5:14.5:18:21.5:25) cm in st st beg with a K row, ending with a WS row.
Shape armhole
Cast off 3 sts at beg next 2 rows.
Dec 1 st at each end of next 3(3:3:3:4:4:4:4:4) rows and 0(0:0:0:3:3:3:3:3) foll alt rows.
(41:47:53:59:53:59:65:73:81)sts)
Cont without further shaping until work measures 13(13:14:15:15.5:18:18:20:20) cm from beg armhole shaping ending with a WS row.
Shape shoulders and back neck
Cast off 3(4:5:6:4:5:6:7:8) sts at beg next 2 rows.
Cast off 3(4:5:6:5:5:6:7:9) sts, K8(9:9:10:9:10:11:12:13), turn leaving rem sts on a holder.
Work each side of neck separately.
Cast off 4 sts, work to end.
Cast off rem 4(5:5:6:5:6:7:8:9) sts.
With RS facing rejoin yarn to rem sts, cast off centre 13(13:15:15:17:19:19:21:21) sts, K to end.
Complete to match first side reversing shaping.

POCKET LININGS (3rd, 4th, 5th, 6th, 7th, 8th & 9th sizes only)
Cast on 17(17:19:19:19:21:21) sts and work
12(14:14:16:16:18:18) rows in st st ending with a WS row.
Leave sts on a holder.

LEFT FRONT
Cast on 26(29:32:35:36:39:42:46:50) sts using 4mm (US 6) needles and cont in st st as folls:
3rd(4th:5th:6th:7th:8th & 9th sizes only)
Work 12(14:14:16:16:18:18) rows in st st beg with a K row.
Place pocket
K7(9:8:10:11:12:14), slip next 17(17:19:19:19:21:21) sts onto a holder and K across first pocket lining, K to end.
All sizes
Work in st st until front matches back to armhole shaping ending with a WS row.
Shape armhole
Cast off 3 sts at beg next row.
Work 1 row.
Dec 1 st at armhole edge on next 3(3:3:3:4:4:4:4:4) rows and 0(0:0:0:3:3:3:3:3) foll alt rows.
(20(23:26:29:26:29:32:36:40)sts)
Cont without further shaping until front is 5(5:7:7:9:9:11:11:11) rows shorter then back to shoulder shaping ending with a RS row.
Shape front neck
Cast off 4 sts at beg next row and foll alt row.
Dec 1 st at neck edge on next 2(2:3:3:4:5:5:6:6) rows.
(10(13:15:18:14:16:19:22:26)sts)
Cont without further shaping until front matches back to shoulder shaping.
Shape shoulder
Cast off 3(4:5:6:4:5:6:7:8) sts, at beg next row and 3(4:5:6:5:5:6:7:9) sts beg foll alt row.
Work 1 row.
Cast off rem 4(5:5:6:5:6:7:8:9) sts.

RIGHT FRONT
Work as for left front reversing shaping and placing of pockets where applicable.

SLEEVES (both alike)
Cast on 27(27:29:33:33:37:37:41:41) sts using 3^1/$_4$mm (US 3) needles and work in **moss st** as folls:
Row 1 (RS): (K1, P1) to last st K1.
Rep this row 3(3:5:5:5:5:5:5:5) times more.
Change to 4mm (US 6) needles and cont in st st beg with a K row, inc 1 st at each end of 1st row and every foll 4th row to 55(57:49:41:51:51:41:51:51) sts and then for **3rd, 4th, 5th, 6th, 7th, 8th & 9th** sizes every foll 6th row to 57(63:63:71:71:81:81) sts.
(55(57:57:63:63:71:71:81:81)sts)
Cont without further shaping until sleeve measures 22(23.5:26.5:30:32:34:39:42:44)cm or length required from cast on edge ending

with a WS row.
Shape sleeve head
Cast off 3 sts at beg next 2 rows.
Dec 1 st at each end of next row and 2(2:2:2:4:4:4:4:4) foll alt rows.
Cast off rem 43(45:45:51:47:55:55:65:65) sts.

MAKING UP
PRESS all pieces as described on the information page.
Join both shoulder seams using back stitch. Sew sleeves into place and join side and sleeve seams (see information page).
Lace edging
Cast on 9 sts using 4mm (US 6) needles and work lace edging as folls:
Row 1: K2, (yon, K2tog) twice, yon, K3.
Row 2 & all WS rows: Knit.
Row 3: K2, (yon, K2tog) twice, yon, K4.
Row 5: K2, (yon, K2tog) twice, yon, K5.
Row 7: K2, (yon, K2tog) twice, yon, K6.
Row 9: K2, (yon, K2tog) twice, yon, K7.
Row 11: K2, (yon, K2tog) twice, yon, K8.
Row 12: Cast off 6 sts, K8. (9sts)
Rep rows 1 - 12 until edging is long enough to fit around bottom edge of garment, leave sts on a holder.
Slip st into place, adjust length, cast off.
Buttonband
Cast on 5 sts using 3^1/$_4$mm (US 3) needles and work in **moss st** until band fit up left front to beg neck shaping when slightly stretched, leave sts on a holder, slip stitch into place.
Mark position of 4(4:4:4:5:5:5:6:6) buttons the first to come 1.5cm from cast on edge, the last will come 1cm into neck band, the rem spaced evenly between.
Buttonhole band
Work as for button band with the addition of 3(3:3:3:4:4:4:5:5) buttonholes worked as to correspond with markers as folls and ending with a WS row:
Buttonhole row: Patt 2, yon, patt 2tog, patt 1.
Neck band
With RS of right front facing and using 3^1/$_4$mm (US 3) needles patt 5 sts from holder, pick up and K14(14:14:14:16:18:18:19:19) sts up right front neck, 21(21:23:23:25:27:27:29:29) sts across back neck, 14(14:14:14:16:18:18:19:19) sts down left front neck, patt across 5 sts from holder.
(59(59:61:61:67:73:73:77:77)sts)
Work 4 row in **moss st**, working buttonhole as before on 2nd row.
Cast off in **moss st**.
Pocket tops
Slip sts from holder onto a 3 1/4mm (US 3) needle and work 4 rows in **moss st**.
Cast off in **moss st**.
See information page for finishing instructions.

Information page

TENSION

Obtaining the correct tension is extremly important. It controls both the shape and size of an article, so any variation, however slight, can distort the finished look of the garment. We strongly advise that you knit a square in pattern and or stocking stitch (depending on the pattern instruction) of perhaps 5 - 10 more stitches and 5 - 10 more rows than those given in the tension note. Place the finished square on a flat surface and measure the central area. If you have too many stitches to 10cm try again using thicker needles, if you have too few stitches to 10cm try again using finer needles. Once you have achieved the correct tension your garment will be knitted to the measurements given in the pattern.

SIZE NOTE

The instructions are given for the smallest size. Where they vary, work the figures in brackets for the larger sizes. One set of figures refers to all sizes. For ease in reading charts it may be helpful to have the chart enlarged at a printers and then to outline the size you intend to knit on the chart.

CHART NOTE

Many of the patterns in the book are worked from charts. Each square on a chart represents a stitch and each line of squares a row of knitting. When working from the charts, read odd rows (K) from right to left and even rows (P) from left to right, unless otherwise stated. Each colour used is given a different symbol or letter and these are shown in the **materials** section, or in the **key** alongside the chart of each pattern.

KNITTING WITH COLOUR

There are two main methods of working colour into a knitted fabric: **Intarsia** and **Fairisle** techniques. The first method produces a single thickness of fabric and is usually used where a colour is only required in a particular area of a row and does not form a repeating pattern across the row, as in the fairisle technique.

Intarsia: The simplest way to do this is to cut short lengths of yarn for each motif or block of colour used in a row. Then joining in the various colours at the appropriate point on the row, link one colour to the next by twisting them around each other where they meet on the wrong side to avoid gaps. All ends can then either be darned along the colour join lines, as each motif is completed or then can be "knitted-in" to the fabric of the knitting as each colour is worked into the pattern. This is done in much the same way

as "weaving-in" yarns when working the Fairisle technique and does save time darning-in ends. It is essential that the tension is noted for **Intarsia** as this may very from the stocking stitch if both are used in the same pattern.

Fairisle type knitting: When two or three colours are worked repeatedly across a row, strand the yarn **not** in use loosely behind the stitches being worked. If you are working with more than two colours, treat the "floating" yarns as if they were one yarn and always spread the stitches to their correct width to keep them elastic. It is advisable not to carry the stranded or "floating" yarns over more than three stitches at a time, but to weave them under and over the colour you are working. The "floating" yarns are therefore caught at the back of the work.

ALL ribs should be knitted to a firm tension, for some knitters it may be necessary to use a smaller needle.

PRESSING

After working for hours knitting a garment, it is worthwhile taking extra time and care on pressing and finishing your garment. After darning in all the ends, block each piece of knitting. Press each piece, except ribs, gently, using a warm iron over a damp cloth. Take special care to press the edges as this will make the sewing up both easier and neater.

FINISHING INSTRUCTIONS

When stitching the pieces together match the colour patterns very carefully. Use a back stitch for all main knitting seams and an edge to edge stitch for all ribs unless otherwise stated.
Join left shoulder seam using back stitch and neckband seam (where appropriate) using an edge to edge stitch.

Sleeves
Set in sleeves: Set in sleeve easing sleeve head into armhole using back stitch.
Square set in sleeve: Set sleeve head into armhole, the straight sides at top of sleeve to form a neat right-angle to cast off sts at armhole on back and front, using back stitch.
Straight cast off sleeve: Place centre of cast off edge of sleeve to shoulder seam. Sew in sleeve using back stitch using markers as guidelines where applicable.
Join side and sleeve seams using back stitch.
Slip stitch pocket edgings and linings into place.
Sew on buttons to correspond with buttonholes.
After sewing up, press seams and hems. Ribbed welts and neckbands and any areas of garter stitch should **not be pressed.**

ABBREVIATIONS

K	knit
P	purl
st(s)	stitch(es)
inc	increase(ing)
dec	decrease(ing)
st st	stocking stitch (1 row K, 1 row P)
beg	begin(ning)
foll	following
folls	follows
rem	remain(ing)
rev	reverse(ing)
rep	repeat
alt	alternate
cont	continue
patt	pattern
tog	together
mm	millimetres
cm	centimetres
in(s)	inch(es)
RS	right side
WS	wrong side
psso	pass slip stitch over
tbl	through back loop
sl	slip
M1	make one stitch by picking up horizontal loop before next stitch and knitting into back of it
yo & yon	yarn over needle
yf	yarn forward
yb	yarn back
yrn	yarn round needle
cn	cable needle
RH	right hand needle
LH	left hand needle

YARN CONVERSION

4-ply wool
Rowan True 4-ply Botany

Double knitting wool
Rowan Designer D.K.

Aran-weight
Rowan Magpie
Rowan Magpie Naturals
Rowan Magpie Tweed

Chunky wool
Rowan Chunky Tweed
Rowan Recycled

Double knitting cotton
Rowan Handknit D.K. cotton
Rowan Den-m-nit (allow for shrinkage)

Stockist Information

For details of U.K. stockist or any other information concerning this book please contact:

Rowan Yarns
Green Lane Mill
Holmfirth
Huddersfield
West Yorkshire
HD7 1EA

Tel: 01484 681881
Fax: 01484 687920

OVERSEAS DISTRIBUTORS

AUSTRALIA
Rowan (Australia)
191 Canterbury Road
Canterbury
Victoria 3126

Tel: (03) 830 1609
Fax: (03) 888 5658

BELGIUM
Hedera
Pleinstraat 68
3001 Leuven

Tel: (016) 23 21 89
Fax: (016) 23 59 97

CANADA
Estelle Designs & Sales Ltd
Units 65/67
2220 Midland Ave
Scarborough
Ontario
M1P 3E6

Tel: (416) 298 9922
Fax: (416) 298 2429

DENMARK
Designer Garn
Vesterbro 33 A
DK-9000 Aalborg

Tel: (98) 13 48 24
Fax: (98) 13 02 13

FRANCE
Elle Tricote
52 Rue Principale
67300 Schiltigheim (Strasbourg)

Tel: (88) 62 65 31
Fax: (88) 18 92 02

GERMANY
Wolle & Design
Wolfshovener Strasse 76
52428 Julich-Stettemich

Tel: 02461 54735
Fax: 02461 4535

HOLLAND
Henk & Henrietta Beukers
Dorpsstraat 9
NL-5327 AR Hurwenen

Tel: 04182 1764
Fax: 04182 2532

ICELAND
Storkurinn
Kjorgardi
Laugavegi 59
ICE-101 Reykjavik

Tel: (01) 18258
Fax: (01) 628252

ITALY
La Compagnia Del Cotone
Via Mazzini 44
I-10123 Torino

Tel (011) 87 83 81

JAPAN
Diakeito Co Ltd
2-3-11 Senba-Higashi
Minoh City
Osaka 562

Tel: 0727 27 6604
Fax: 0727 27 6654

NEW ZEALAND
John Q Goldingham Ltd
P O Box 45083
Epuni Railway
Lower Hutt

Tel: (04) 5674 085 or (04) 5674 094
Fax: (04) 5697 444

NORWAY
Eureka
P O Box 357
N-1401 Ski

Tel: (64) 86 55 44
Fax: (64) 86 55 41

SWEDEN
Wincent
Sveavagen 94
113 50 Stockholm

Tel: (08) 673 70 60
Fax: (08) 673 31 71

U S A
Westminster Trading Corporation
5 Northern Boulevard
Amherst
New Hampshire 03031

Tel: (603) 886 5041/5043
Fax: (603) 886 1056

Acknowledgements

First a big thank you to all our wonderful models for looking so brilliant and making Tadpoles & Tiddlers so much fun to make. Alexander Booth, Daniel Dyson, Ella Squires, Zoe Green, Maddie Bazuin, Charlie and Harry Rowland, Georgia Wilson, Lilly Beardsell, Daisy and Meredith Hollingworth, Leoni, Liane, Michael Hirst, Zoe and Sam Carr, Joe Bostock, Meggie Laybourn, Jack and Holly Rumbold, Grace Pinner, Beth Sheard and Daisy, Charlotte, Alice and Kate Hughes. Also, thank you to all their parents for being so patient and putting up with all the chaos and to Pam Robinson for loan of 'Fudgie'.

We would like to express our gratitude to David and Hilary Hughes for being so enthusiastic about this book and for allowing us to invade their lives, home and garden.

And last but not least to the Rowan team for their encouragment and in particular to Elizabeth Armitage and her team of knitters who all worked so hard to produce the beautifully knitted garments.